Be the Woman You Want To Be

Ruthe White

Harvest House Publishers
Irvine, California 92714

Foreword

Today's woman can be whatever she wants to be! In this day of new liberation for women, she can enter the competitive business world and be anything from a truck driver to a politician. Or, she can more skillfully develop the qualities that have been attached to the female sex as a seamstress, gourmet cook or interior designer. She has been hoodwinked into believing that all of this new potential for women will open the doors to a more fulfilling world.

With the new freedom comes the encouragement to gain her independence and to demand her equal rights. Often bit by bit, she begins to be influenced and pulled in a direction that is totally unfamiliar to her. I know this is true because I have found myself on several occasions caught up in the whirlwind of women's independence and rights. It is only when we come in out of the storm and examine what God says about women, that we can recognize the right direction to go.

Ruthe White very superbly causes us to examine who we are, who we want to be and where we are going.

The spiritual woman will first consider what does God want her to be and then will want to become that woman. True fulfillment only comes when we set our hearts and professions in line with Jesus Christ.

Beverly La Haye

Acknowledgements

To these . . .

. . . My husband, who by some form of osmosis, transmitted a part of his courage to me. Without his masculine strength, and support, this manuscript would still be playing "hide-and-seek" with my ailing ego, and left hidden in the cardboard box where it was originally filed.

. . . Our daughters, Deanna and Jan, for having taught me about life, how to live, laugh, and the joy of loving. Their tender relationship with me was the source of inspiration which "prodded" me into the field of journalism.

. . . My friends who gave of themselves so willingly in the editing, typing, and proofreading of this book; particularly to Brenda Harris, the copy editor.

. . . I want to say:

"THANKS"

Sponsor a
BEAUTY OF WOMANHOOD SEMINAR.

Use this book as your text.

Write:

Mrs. Ruthe White
331 Mc Creary
Hanford, Ca. 93230

BE THE WOMAN YOU WANT TO BE

Copyright © 1978 Harvest House Publishers
Irvine, California 92714
Library of Congress Catalog Card Number: 77-88190
ISBN 0-89081-114-8

All rights reserved. No portion of this book may be
reproduced in any form without the written
permission of the publisher.

Printed in the United States of America.

Contents

Unit I

Who Are You?

1

Who Is the
20th Century Woman?

Have you ever felt like the elasticity of your endurance was being stretched to the breaking point? Then, join the club with millions of other women who are caught between the demands of day-to-day living, and the fast moving trends of our culture.

The twentieth century woman is caught in the "gravitational" pull of a society whose demands upon her are like a game of "tug of war."

One segment of today's women is yelling its head off for freedom, equal rights, unisex, and complete independence; on the other end of the spectrum, there is a strong move, among our more saintly (whatever that is) women, to give us no privileges other than those handed to us by our own Mr. Adam.

Out of these widely varying extremes there is a great vacuum developing, a sense of psychological pressure, and . . . the twentieth century woman has become the target; yet, she must remain calm, cool and collected, as she is exploited, glamorized, and spiritualized.

The Christian woman has yet another problem: She is told that she must maintain an hourglass figure (and I'm for that if you can do it), and be as versed in world affairs as a well-known woman news commentator. She must be a "Boudoir Evangelist" to her husband at all times. A woman for "all seasons!" All of these qualities, they tell us, will be the by-product of their pat formulas for instant success.

I don't believe it!

We are the "battering ram!" The feminists say: "Take off all restraints." Theologians keep reminding us of our "yoke of bondage" to complete submission. As a result of all these conflicting ideologies, we have know-how-manuals on everything from sex to sainthood. These encyclopedias of do's and don'ts are, of course, helpful. But they can also prove to be frustrating! We must admit that somewhere between complete independence and total submission the woman is left "dangling."

I can accept all these varied opinions as being valid within a "scale of balance." But, once a great truth is revealed, it seems to be human nature to take it as "the method," without understanding it as being part of the whole. Then, we get ourselves all out of "whack" again and spend our lifetime in getting back into balance.

Now, it is not my point to argue philosophies with the more intellectual sisters of my day, nor to de-emphasize the role of the spiritual woman. Rather, I should like to remind ourselves, and others, that we are human! Because we are, and because we live in a realistic world, we cannot be rolled up into neat little packages and labeled with spiritual euphoria. I don't think any of us will ever become a composite picture of all the biblical women tied into one human frame. In fact, there is a question in my mind as to whether God would want us to.

Let me ask you: "How can you be creative, within the framework of God's plan for your life, if you are always feeling like you are being stretched tighter than a violin string, or wound up like an eight-day clock?"

Listen—when the oxygen of your inner self is so stifled you are beginning to feel like a corseted woman, about to break out all over—you had better watch out! That is exactly what is happening in our society. This constant bombardment is producing a syndrome of extreme-"ism," "uptightness," and a never quite-satisfied feeling of inadequacy.

We are conditioned to expect and feel that we must be perfect in every detail of life. Is it because of our tendency to try and meet all the demands being laid upon us by society and the religious world?

If so, perhaps the time has come for us to examine ourselves in the perspective of who we are under God. Nowhere do I find this feeling in relation to Him!

Look at the motley crew our Lord chose! They were far from perfection. Yet, He entrusted His entire ministry into their unskilled hands. Blundering Peter, the biblical apostle, was allowed to make his own mistakes; but, he knew the thrill of both failure and success. He went under, trying to walk on the water, and came up being led by the Master's hand. So, there comes a time in each of our lives, when we have to leave others in the boat of life situations, and strike out on a daring step into life's sea, knowing full well, there are risks involved. We don't have to know everything about the Lord before starting, just recognize the voice of the Master and head toward Him.

Faith always has to come to a place of total abandonment to oneself.

ILLUSTRATION:

When our younger daughter, Jan, was about three years old, she developed a very bad habit of climbing. It really didn't matter what, so long as she could climb it. One day as her father entered the room, he walked past a chair she had just crawled up into. As he came near her she jumped straight up, threw both arms into the air, and leaped toward him. His natural impulse was to reach out and catch her. Which he did! (I think another was to spank her for such a dangerous act.) In any event, the child felt the need for total self-abandonment, knowing full well her father would catch her before the fall.

I am not talking to you about doing such a foolish and perhaps, childish act; rather, to encourage you to have trust in the *heavenly Father*, who will not let you fall—even when you may not fully understand the dangers!

Remember, God still leads the individual! He works through the circumstances of your life to guide you into new dimensions of spiritual growth. He may, or may not, want to use you in any prescribed pattern, since no two of us live in the same sterile atmosphere.

Now, I am not suggesting you disregard workable principles in God's Word. However, I speak of your individual right to a rediscovery of yourself, to find a balance between the major philosophical extremes as they affect you; and, of your privilege to examine the direction in which the present trends are taking you.

What are these trends?

They are, as I see them: *Women's Extremist Groups* and *Spiritual Idealism*. Most of us, as women, are caught somewhere in the middle of the two, having only a vague understanding of the undercurrent that is pulling at us. It is for that reason I have chosen to look at the profile of the *women extremists* first, hoping you may be prodded into a more in-depth study of how this extreme affects you personally. We will then discuss the other end of the spectrum, *idealism*, before looking at ourselves as the women in the middle, in need of balance.

2

Extremes:
To Be or Not to Be?

The feminists are women with goals—and they know where they want to go! These women are coming out of the kitchen woodwork, shedding their stereotyped aprons of past identity, going into every known vocation from car racing to politics. They are knocking on the ecclesiastical doors of the religious world, forcing attention upon themselves as equal, and demanding equality for all persons.

That is, equality as they see it. To some of us, there is a question as to what that is, in terms of what we see happening. However, they have gone out after the business world, forcing them to take a good hard look at our innate abilities.

Now, I know some of you are already saying: "That doesn't affect me!" But let me tell you, "It does." What one of us would not like to receive equal pay for equal work? We all would!

So, don't pull your spiritual maxi-skirt around you, thinking yourself immune to the effects of their ideology. No one is! Whether you are male or female,

Christian or non-Christian, you are—and will be—affected.

No spiritual inoculation will prevent the virus of these groups from spreading. Could it be that is one of our problems? While we, "saint-and-not-too-saintly" ones, have ridden our spiritual merry-go-rounds, the extremists have been playing music on another carousel. Believe me, their tune is being heard! Some of us have run in our religious circles, too busy to get involved. While we have slept, they have sown strange seeds in our backyards, on the playgrounds of our schools, and in the minds of a new generation of youth. Now, we are being faced with the problem of what to do about the situation.

Is this what Jesus meant when He said,

> . . . the children of this world are in
> their generation wiser than the chil-
> dren of light. Luke 16:8 KJV.

Perhaps it is time we took a good hard look at ourselves in relation to the world around us. It could be that only the tip of the "iceberg of lib" has surfaced.

I will be the first to admit, when the first few women started speaking out for the extremist movements, that I laughed into my oversized coffee mug and asked myself: "I wonder who they think they are?" Well! It's different now. I don't believe they, themselves, were aware of the tremendous impact they were bringing into our culture.

Betty Friedan, feminist leader states:

> Originally I had projected it would take
> 25 years for the Feminist movement to

sweep the world. Instead, it has required only 10 years for lib to sweep America. It is the only revolution known in the history of the world where the person who started it lived to see it develop.

What about this potential "cyclone" of change? Let's hear the answer from the mouth of the leaders themselves. When asked about their goals and objectives, this is a profile of what they perceived for the future.

WHAT IS WOMEN'S LIB?

FACT:	PREDICTIONS:	GOALS:
1. The feminist group is like a watershed. It is sweeping across the United States.	1. A wave current of groups will join forces to shape American politics.	1. To promote equal rights for all persons.
2. Their impact is yet to be fully realized.	2. The movements will become a great voting block politically.	2. To apply pressure on the news media for a broader acceptance of all persons.
	3. Gay Liberalists' Women's Lib and Lesbian groups were named as those forming the coalition.	3. To create a powerful enough voting block to make legislative changes in their favor.

——as stated by:
Elaine Noble, Feminist leader and member of Mass. Legislature, on the "Tomorrow Show," Feb. 11, 1975.

An example of this can be seen in the article published by the *San Francisco Chronicle*, and written by Michael Grieg, on a proposed program for sex education, as viewed by the liberation movement.

> See Dick run. See Jane run.
> Dick and Jane are running into
> each other's arms.
> Dick is making love to Jane.
> Jane is loving it.
> See Jane smile. See Dick smile. [1]

He describes the breezy humor and explicit language the primer uses, as it was being written for supplemental classroom usage. The self-styled sex course for kids, according to Grieg, was being designed with paste-ups of the human anatomy to accelerate the learning procedure.

While this book may, or may not, come into the schools, it is nevertheless an indication of what can be expected from the liberation front. (I am wondering how many of us would know, or be aware, if it were being used now.)

Not only are we feeling the impact of "lib" in these areas, but the twentieth century woman is caught with the problem of knowing just where to get off or on this fast moving escalator of trends. Her children are also struggling with it! We all face the threat against the very God image, of our religious training, as it is being challenged by them.

The *Los Angeles Times*, carried an article written by John Dart entitled: *Feminists Challenging God-the-Father Image.* In this article, Mr. Dart states:

> Jesus as feminist is just one of the new
> perspectives on the woman's image in

1. Michael Grieg, San Francisco *Chronicle*, January 13, 1975.

the Bible, and the recreation of God in a male-female image emerging from theological and academic circles.

The growing numbers of women and seminary students are doing most of the work—which includes suggestions to avoid such male-oriented hymns as "God Rest Ye Merry Gentlemen" and initial steps to produce a non-sexist translation of the Bible . . . [2]

Bud Kepler, director of ministerial studies at Harvard Divinity School, says:

Rather than continue to see Eve as a culprit in the fall from favor 'we ought to celebrate Eve.' She began the process of freedom.

This same spirit is being carried over into other areas of the theological world. In June, 1974, Nelle Morton told a World Council of Churches meeting on woman's status, "There is no God language free from sexist imagery." Books presenting new worship services and prayers omitting exclusive male descriptions of God were published by two campus ministers, Sharon and Thomas Neufer Emswiler.

Reverend Nancy Self, in speaking of the role of the feminists in religion, says:

. . . the movement for equal rights is a sign of the Holy Spirit at work in our midst.

2. John Dart, Los Angeles *Times*, December 29, 1974.

Again, simply ignoring what is happening will not make it go away. The time has come for us, as twentieth century women, to begin speaking out for ourselves. We need to get involved, see what is happening around us, and begin to be heard.

It is not my purpose to give you answers, but I should like to prod you into doing some thinking for yourself about where you fit.

Let us begin by asking the question: "Is women's lib all bad, or some good?" Listed below are a few points you might wish to consider in your analysis.

IS WOMEN'S LIB GOOD OR BAD?

GOOD	BAD
1. We have better working conditions for the working woman.	1. Women are succumbing to diseases which were once more common to the male. (Heart, ulcer, arterial.)
2. There is a much fuller recognition of the woman's role, her potential and individual rights.	2. Home pressures are building within the family structure as to husband/wife roles.
3. There is much greater acceptance of the woman in every segment of society.	3. Women working at jobs are presenting an identity crisis between spouses.
	4. There is subtle conditioning for women to build their own independence.
	5. A growing climate is producing acceptance of amoral practices.

ALONG WITH ALL THIS THRUST FROM THE FEMINIST GROUPS——THERE ARE SOME VERY IMPORTANT QUESTIONS FOR YOUR CONSIDERATION!

Ask yourself:

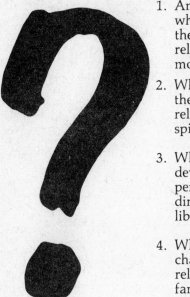

1. Am I informed about what is happening in the world around me in relation to these movements?

2. When did I last evaluate the changes as they relate to my individual spirit life? (Lib)

3. What changes do I see developing in my own personal life-style, as a direct result of women's lib?

4. Where do I suspect these changes will lead me in relation to my home, family, others?

5. What am I doing to reinforce myself in a positive way, against negative trends?

Write it out:_____

_____

List the major changes you can observe as a result of "women's lib."

Home			Personally		
	good	bad		good	bad
1.	_____	_____	1.	_____	_____
2.	_____	_____	2.	_____	_____
3.	_____	_____	3.	_____	_____

Society
good   bad

1. _____   _____

2. _____   _____

3. _____   _____

List the last three books you read:

1. _____ 2. _____
_____ 3. _____

    Are these books making you aware of what is happening around you?
    Did the books you read give information? Challenge?_____ Encouragement?_____Discouragement?_____

    Below is one woman's reply to the twentieth century extremism . . .

"I AM A WOMAN"

I like being a woman . . .
    I would be the first to admit that it would be easier
        if . . .
            There were no menstrual cramps,
            Labor pains in delivery,
            No menopausal changes.
So what? According to statistics . . .
    I stand the chance of outliving my husband for at
        least three years, perhaps seven.
Every women's libber yells her head off for
    freedom . . .

Equal rights.
She begs to be accepted as a person,
Tells of her search for identity,
Declares her rights to act, dress, and live in so-
called complete freedom.
What is this freedom?
Is it a freedom of identity, or a liberation to
conformity?
Why the big deal?
Personally . . .
I wish all of them would wear their labels.
At least, I would be able to tell them from the men.
I have never been a person who wished to remain
neutral on the important issues of life.
Certainly . . .
Not in my status as a woman!
I want to live, act and dress like a woman, like a
lady if you please. Knowing the style of clothing,
whether casual or formal, does not in itself make
me a lady, but *the lady* inside the garment makes
the difference, and her identity must never be
lost.
Pray tell me . . .
If the women's "libbers" dislike men so much, why
do they try to be so much like them?
Why is it so important to them, to conform with
such masculine mannerism of dress and action?
Why do they propound the causes of lesbianism?
I am confused . . .
Confused over this banter for freedom.
I want freedom too . . .
Freedom that gives me privileges and responsibilities. Let the so-called liberated woman yell her
head off about the idea of fidelity being absurd,
about promiscuity being the "in thing."

She can talk about . . .
Shaping the American politics,
Flaunt her sex life on television, in movies and magazines,
And try to change laws for the legalization of dope, and prostitution.
But I say . . . "Hold it, Sister."
I, too, want to shape American politics!
Let me begin in my home to teach Christian principles around my family altar.
Maybe I have slept while you sowed your wild seeds,
But watch out, for here I come.
Don't minimize my role as a mother, who skillfully molds the mind of her young child.
I want to love one husband . . . freely and openly, to respect him as a person, a part of me. You can have your independence. I like being a part of warmth that comes in holding hands with the man I can trust, and in the security of knowing he trusts me.
So . . .
Do not take away my liberty to live under God as a free person!
Do not try and force me, by social pressure, to take up your mantle, in the name of social justice.
I had . . .
Freedom before you came along—an inner freedom—a freedom of conscience between myself and God.

SUGGESTED READING MATERIAL AS TO WHAT WOMEN'S LIB IS:

Hole, Judith and Ellen Levine. *Rebirth of Feminism.* New York: Quadrangle Books, 1973.

Koedt, Anne, ed. *Radical Feminism*. New York: Quadrangle Books, 1973.

ARGUMENTS AGAINST WOMEN'S LIB:

Beardsley, Lou and Toni Spry. *The Fulfilled Woman*. Irvine, California: Harvest House Publishers, 1975.

Chandler, Sandra. *The Sensitive Woman*. Irvine, California: Harvest House Publishers, 1972.

Morgan, Marabel. *Total Woman*. Old Tappan, N.J.: Fleming H. Revell Co., 1973.

Stanssinopoulos, Arianna. *The Female Woman*. Pittsburgh, Pa: Know Inc., 1974.

3

What of
Religious Idealism?

These pseudo/spiritual women come in all sizes and shapes. They come from every theological segment of the religious world. Their song is a different one, the melody is familiar, but the lyrics sound strange.

So many women are joining in on the chorus, we can no longer point a finger of accusation at a particular sect or cult and label them as the Grand Choirmaster. (Thus, we cannot lay credit, or blame.) These women move back and forth between denominational pews, like playing a game of musical chairs. (Which is not to say it is bad!)

With this shift in religious thinking has come overtones of great spiritual extremes. Perhaps that is a good thing! At least it has brought, and is bringing, a *counter balance* between the two major philosophies of "women's liberation groups" and "idealism."

However, it is unfortunate that in so doing, a few women have set themselves up as spiritual authorities. There has been a rise of *"pat religious"* formulas for instant success. The *"idealists"* make a game of giving simplistic answers to earthshaking problems. Once they have introduced a good principle, it seems to automatically become a law unto itself. To dare question any of these is to bring down a strong hammer of guilt upon one's self.

So, they have us tied in neat little packages. We are labeled and cataloged, tied with bows of spiritual euphoria.

"BOUDOIR EVANGELISM"

We are told that if our homes are to be secure, husbands safe, we must have a revival of *"boudoir evangelism."* "Win your husbands in the bedroom, girls," they yell at us.

C. M. Ward, writes about what he calls "bedroom evangelism." (I thought it interesting from a man's point of view.) He says:

> Male and female believers are being seduced by bits of shabbiness masquerading as Christian "sexperts" who ladle bedroom advice at bestseller prices.

> A new interpretation for the believer's wife is being developed with alluring profit potential to the producers. It's a new packaging. You wrap the charismatic sparkle in today's expression of sex, and hopefully produce the ideal woman . . . The plea to save the believer's marriage with this new formula is alluring: "It is only when a woman surrenders her life to her hus-

band, reveres and worships him, and is
willing to serve him, that she becomes
really beautiful to him.

Mr. Ward makes this observation, and further
states:

> When you cut down into the marrow,
> there's a frightening aspect to this new
> evangelism. It asks the believer's wife
> to assume that every unbeliever-
> husband is essentially unfaithful—that
> believing wives must predicate their
> conduct on this premise since they
> count on the infidelity of their hus-
> bands—which leads to a frantic
> attempt to keep him interested. [3]

Well now, personally, I don't think the idea of
meeting your husband at the door, in sexy attire is
bad at all. But, it is not the *panacea* that cures all the
spiritual, and marital, ills of your home and family!

Isn't it strange! Some of us want to solve all our
problems on our knees, in scroungy bathrobes, and
with unkempt hair. Others set out to win their
victories in the beauty shop, at the lingerie counter,
or in a spa. Why can't we have a balance of both?

SUBMISSION AND BALANCE

A very lovely young woman came to me with this

3. C. M. Ward, "Bedroom Evangelism," Reprinted
from the *Pentecostal Evangel* by permission,
Copyright 1976 by the General Council of the
Assemblies of God, February 8, 1976.

story not long ago. She said: For three years I have catered to the "whims" of my husband, whose domineering actions soon became unbearable. The more I gave in to him the more he demanded of me. It was impossible for me to be true to my inner convictions; but, I was trying to follow the formula of total surrender unto my husband, for the sake of his spiritual life.

Fatigue and inner resentment began to take hold of me. I was a "seething saint in a robe of piety." Outwardly there was surrender; internally, I was dying, both spiritually and psychologically. Finally I began to understand some of the principles of balance, and this is what I discovered.

1. Submission must begin toward God, as a child of the heart.

2. A woman under God's authority will want to bring the other areas of her life into balance with God's principles.

   a) To verbally submit to anyone, without an honest willingness to do so, brings inner hostilities.

   b) Submission is more than surface piety.

   c) It is not the loss of self-identity, but a **recognition of another's identity**.

3. When husband, others, or governmental authority, go against God's Word, there can **never** be submission to both God and them.

   a) God never works against Himself.

   b) Nor does He allow the Christian woman to indulge in sinful practices under—**the banner of submission**.

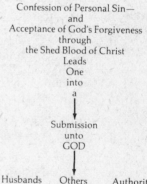

Confession of Personal Sin—
and
Acceptance of God's Forgiveness
through
the Shed Blood of Christ
Leads
One
into
a

Submission
unto
GOD

Husbands   Others   Authority
Eph.5:22   Eph. 5:21   Heb. 13:17

in
Perfect Balance

IDEALISM VS. PRACTICAL-DOWN-TO-EARTH

We must understand there are no easy "hocus-pocus" formulas that can guarantee the very same results in every situation. Our spiritual development comes in finding a balance. How?

Opportunities for self-fulfillment come in the down-to-earth practical things of life. Too many of us overlook the ordinary things while searching for the sublime. Even then, there just does not seem to be any other way for learning, except as we go through our own life experiences.

This personal confession may help you to better understand what I am saying. You see, I am investigative by nature. I want to know the details. What are the intricate workings of a group? And what can I learn from a given situation?

This is the very thing that causes my problem. When the new "fad" of religious and secular books about the woman's role flooded the market I bought them—and tried to apply the principles I felt were in balance with my inner self.

What really happened is: I caught myself on a spiritual merry-go-round, going in circles! About the time I thought one formula was down pat, and I was comfortable with it, another new idea would emerge.

You should know my "not-so-good-nature" kept the spiritual balloon of my life deflated, a lot of the time. I found myself needing to go back to a biblical balance, to understand how God would have me apply those "new ideas" into my own thinking.

I had to screen out and measure what I was learning, with other Scriptures. Since I was always having to come back to the Bible, I began to draw firm convictions about the constant need to check myself for *balance*!

I learned that God has many methods, and I must not "box Him in." Also, he often raises up people to present a neglected truth, but He never intended it should be a law unto itself.

For instance, "theology in the bedroom," is alright with me, but the bedroom is only one of several rooms in my house. What do I do when the refrigerator breaks down, and the washer has flooded the kitchen floor? Running to an encyclopedia of "do's and don'ts" will not help! Even "praising the Lord" is not going to solve the problem. (It *will* help you get through it!)

If I am helped I must get with it: deal with the difficulty as it arises; tackle the problems of life even when they hurt (and life does hurt); and understand that growth comes, not in rationalizing and/or spirtualizing the problem away, but in facing up to it. Maturity is growth, right in the *middle* of the problem. This is true whether it is in cleaning up a flooded kitchen floor or a messy typewriter ribbon, or in living with an unbelieving spouse.

Is this what Paul was speaking about in Rom. 5:1-5?

I grant you this Scripture is being paraphrased, and it is according to my translation—but this is the way I read it:

> Because I have peace with God through our Lord Jesus Christ, and faith in His *grace*, I stand (right in the middle of the water soaked floor) rejoicing (not in what is happening but . . .) in the *hope* of God's glory.

Not only so, but know (that out of this mess) I am learning *patience*.

And *patience* cannot be learned without *experience* (Lord, you know this really is a mess), and *experience* brings *hope* (hope it won't happen again.)

For *hope* is not something that makes me ashamed (i.e., ashamed to admit that I had the experience); because that is the very thing that is proving God's love is shed abroad in my heart.

This Scripture gives me a spiritual stance because:

a. I have identified my position under grace;
b. Understood that grace is not affected by external circumstances; and,
c. I am still under grace while right in the middle of the problem.

FORMULA:

Peace with God + Faith in His grace + Rejoicing in His Word = Patience

Knowledge + Experience = Hope

Hope + Unashamed Confession of Faith + God's Love = Growth

READ: Eph. 2:6-10 ("Sitting with God")

What about you? Are you troubled about your position under God, as it relates to problem areas of your life? Why not stop here, and have a chat with God about what is "bugging you."

A PRAYER FOR "TROUBLED SAINTS"

Lord, I believe in your ability to help *me*, as an individual. I personally accept your forgiveness, by the confession of my sins, and faith in your shed blood.

I know you love me! Because of this love, you will give me direction and guidance.

Help me, that I will not set out to solve all the problems of my life in one day. I want to learn to trust you for today, knowing that you have promised me help for tomorrow. Lead me step-by-step, just one day at a time.

I know your love is unlimited, your grace abiding. Thanks for the deep sense of security as I rest in you.

Amen

P.S. Lord, remind me of these things when I seem to forget!

4

Who is that Woman in Between?

Women on the move are a common phenomenon in America today. These are upper middle class women who have reached a point in their lives where there is a vague lack of self-fulfillment . . . and are seeking change.

Gerald Self
San Francisco Chronicle

Whether we like it or not a move is on. There is an awakening among women. With this new emphasis, and the extremist ideologies, there is an almost frightening urgency to get out and find one's identity. I ask you, "Have you never felt the temptation to walk out on your responsibilities? To leave the 'whole mess' of household drudgery, or whatever else may be holding you?" Don't tell me you haven't felt that way. We all have at one time or another. Oh, I know no one wants to admit it! But, because it lies smoldering, sometimes hidden, the temptation becomes even greater. There is the desire to be creative that keeps gnawing at your insides. You want better living conditions so you consider finding employment. Along with all this is the nagging impulse to find a kind of self-fulfillment.

There is no question as to these needs for fulfillment. They are very real! We all have them. However, there is a danger in our striking out to find some vague form of self-fulfillment, simply because everyone is doing it. No one should, out of pressure, take off on an unknown path, just because it is the popular thing to do. This is true, whether the pressure comes from the far left of "women's lib," or the far right of "religious idealism."

Mr. Webster defines what an extreme is: "An extreme is two existing opinions at opposing ends, or far away distance." That is one thing, but what about the object or person caught in the pull?

When the twentieth century woman tries to move from where she is presently, to where she wants to go, the stretch can prove to be painful. It can be like a gravitational tug-of-war!

Far left of society
is
"Women's Lib"

Far right of society
is
"Religious Idealism"

Most of us are caught somewhere
in
Between!

The woman who chooses to work, or may be forced to do so, for reasons beyond her control, is a most likely victim to feel the squeeze. The very minute she seeks employment, there are strong repercussions that will come from the traditional right. While she may expect equal pay for equal work, she may not be ready to burn her bra or take up the banner for liberalism. At the same time, she is moving away from the image her peers have made for her. Somewhere in between these two extremes, there must be a place of balance. A self-acceptance, that comes without feelings of self-guilt.

It seems important that we understand no two persons can approach life's changes in exactly the very same manner. What is perceived by one woman as a "cure-all" for her psychological ills, may become the breaking point for another. For example: one woman can handle employment and maintain a good balance, while others of us are not able to do so.

No two of us live in the same environment, nor do we have the same set of circumstances in which we must adjust. One lady may be moving from the radicalism of the 60s to the idealism of the 70s; another may be on the right, struggling to find her balance in a working women's world.

ILLUSTRATION:

Marcia was a girl who had been raised in a very closed church environment. She shared with me her inner conflicts, as they had developed, from having moved away from the usual role of housewife.

"I am not the usual kind of woman," she said. "Not even in terms of my Christian self-image. You see, I am married, have no children; and, at this point, I am not ready to start a family.

"My position as the manager of a well-known specialized firm, means there are many male employees to whom I must give orders.

"Also, my earnings are more than that of my husband.

"Tell me, who am I, in terms of traditional views and cultural advantages?"

It was necessary for me to point out three things to Marcia.

ONE:

She need not accept someone else's planned pattern for her life. But, she must accept personal responsibility under God, for the decisions she makes.

Both she and her husband should come to an agreement about her working.

TWO:

She needs to believe in God's ability to work through her, in the given set of circumstances. Also knowing that when she can no longer give a Christian witness, her priorities are out of balance.

THREE:

She needs to know that God does not measure her worth by any one set of human criteria. That her self-worth is based entirely upon God's acceptance of her as a *person*. She must seek to please Him. If she cannot adjust to the attitude of her peers, and it is affecting her spiritual life, the problem should be resolved—either by quitting her job, or otherwise.

Renee, another young lady, also in her 20s, had a different kind of problem. Having been a part of the 60s, a member of the revolutionist group who was against the established church, she is now trying to make a change. Christ has come into her heart through the confession of her sins, and the new-found experience is a very real thing to her. She is able to accept God's forgiveness, but is struggling for acceptance within the church circle.

"There is internal pressure coming to me from every direction of the church," she said. "I am fighting with the problem of moving from one extreme to another. Ten years of my life were spent in fighting against the organized establishment, religiously and otherwise. I took my liberties, and fought for my individual freedom.

"Today, I find myself trying to get oriented into a stable situation of personal identity. The spiritual extremists tell me I have *no freedom*. They say my rights must be lost in total submission to another. Have I no individual privileges under God?" she asked.

Renee's problem, although unlike Marcia's, was related. Each of the girls had to resolve the question in much the same manner. *How?*

Both women had to be assured of God's total acceptance of them as a *person*.

Each needed to accept God's redemptive work within, as being complete and based entirely upon faith. Their relationship with God rests in a submission to Him first, above all other persons.

They were able to recognize the area of conflict, and deal with it personally, allowing God to bring them into a practical, biblical balance of faith/ submission.

READ: John 4:1-30

Marcia was on the far right, moving left. Renee was on the left, going to the right. Both of them had to be willing to make realistic adjustments, which they did.

Renee is active in a church in Northern California and has adjusted her working hours to a degree of acceptance by herself and her husband.

Marcia is in Southern California, attending a very fundamental church, experiencing a new self-awareness.

They had to understand that growth is not always measurable and should never be measured by another's growth patterns for development.

WHAT ABOUT THE WOMAN WHO IS UNLIKE EITHER OF THESE?

Maybe you are like myself, you were never a person who wanted the *sensational* "binges" of life. Neither did you like to be labeled a "stick in the mud," afraid of a new challenge.

I have always wanted to be out there where the action is. To be honest, I don't like fence riders. The way I see it, a woman ought to "believe something, and know what that something is." Being neutral on important issues and sitting with folded arms of passivity, while the world marches on, is no symbol of Christian piety to me.

Most of my life has been lived among so-called church women. I've watched some ladies dry up in their "spiritual hulls" and crystalize around a safe position. They never put themselves out there where people are; afraid to join a P.T.A. group, too religious to read a current magazine, simply not interested in anything outside their little circle of closed opinions.

Then, there are others, whom I felt had a firm grip on themselves and God, whose attitudes were different. They were not blind to their role in the community, and could identify with the norm of society.

My position, as an inside observer to the "religious circle" is: that we are sometimes "lazy," apathetic about keeping ourselves informed, and sometimes aloof from the real issues of day-to-day living.

This is a day that should challenge us into action. We dare not sit idly by while our children become victims of our own lethargy. We need to get out there and find out what is going on in the political world, raise our voices in protest to pornography, support those in public offices who have respect for Christian ideals, and take a stand with them.

Never—no never—should the extremist speak for us! Like a mighty army, we need to go out conquering, letting our voices be heard. Pray, yes! But these are days when praying is not enough. You should know something about the laws, know who you are voting for, learn the facts, and move into action—both in the prayer closets of your home, and in the community.

PLAN OF ACTION

Climate for growth, and self-identity, is created by the Lord, according to "His" knowledge for each person's ability to grow. If your heart is honest, God will lead you into the acceptance of "His plan" without breaking you.

God never frustrates us—He leads us in plain paths of green pastures.

READ: Col. 2:6-10

Submission should be a child of the heart, an attitude—first toward God, then others.

READ:

1. James 4:7
2. Eph. 5:21-22
3. 1 Pet. 2:13

Probably no Scripture is more directed to women, and right-down-the-middle, than the one in Proverbs. For you passive-and-not-too-passive saints, I suggest you read:

Prov. 31:10-31
1. List the qualities of the woman mentioned here.
2. Does she sound like a spiritual recluse?
3. How does she measure up to Eph. 5:22?
(wives be subject to your husband as to the Lord)

5

What About Trends, Fads and Things?

Life should be more than a game of mental "hopscotch." There comes the time, when as a *growing* person, one should assume a place of personal identity, without having to attach one's self to every new idea that emerges. That is not to say one should be rigidly inflexible to outer change; rather, to have a set of inner principles from which one does not deviate.

There is a big difference between sheer stubbornness and an established stance of what Bob Mumford calls, "soul poise." Again, this is where balance comes in, knowing when to move out in personal growth patterns and distinguishing between passing fads and growing trends.

What is a *trend*?

If we are not careful we will find ourselves becoming a part of every new fad that comes through. Some

TREND:

Inclination to drift in a specified or unspecified direction.

women seem always to be moving from one big "hullabaloo" to another, always fighting for some new cause. Never becoming established in themselves or biblical principles, they never really find themselves!

We become like spectators in the game of life, always waiting for someone else to cheer us on. When one faddish cheerleader runs down, we just move on to another, having no personal anchor of self-identity. Much of our culture is geared to condition us to be onlookers, rather than participants. It is as if we were saying, "Give them another million to entertain us so we won't have to think." The old idea of work and moral ethics being synonomous has become blase'.

In some cases we seem to have lost sight of the beautiful art of knowing self-accomplishment through both failure and success. I say *both*, because it is my feeling that sometimes a temporary failure becomes the "stepping stone" to future success.

Along with this trend toward "spectator-ism" is the tendency to keep "up-rooting" ourselves. We are like plants that never have a chance to grow because of being constantly moved from one container to another. Paul cautioned a group of believers against drifting with trends when he said:

Then we will no longer be like children, forever changing our minds about what we

> believe because someone has something dif-
> ferent, or has cleverly lied to us and made
> the lie sound like the truth. Instead, we will
> lovingly follow the truth at ALL TIMES—
> speaking truly, dealing truly, living truly—
> and so become more and more like Christ.
> Eph. 4:14 American Revised

When the apostle talked about "all times" he was referring to patterns of living; and, a tone of balance is certainly implied. Note, there is a difference between a good idea that becomes a fixed dogma, and a biblical principle that is integrated into one's inner self. The first is like an obsessional drive that keeps pushing at us, an insatiable urge for self-fulfillment through an outside stimulus (force); the other, is most satisfiable and keeps broadening its level of growth. However, there is in a spiritual sense, a temptation on the part of some, to go out after whatever theological fad may be "sweeping" at the moment. Eventually, both of these attitudes of constant running will lead one into what I call a—

SEARCH FOR THE MYSTICAL

When one loses sight of the beauty of the ordinary things of life, one has lost the joy of life itself. Pleasure may become an unfulfilled quest for living, and one's cup of pleasure can never be filled! This is especially true when spiritual values are measured by emotional responses.

Solomon the wise man observed this firsthand. He said:

> "He that loveth pleasure shall be a poor
> man." Prov. 21:17 KJV.

He was not speaking then in terms of monetary wealth, but a condition of soul poverty that comes as a natural consequence to the perpetual pleasure seeker. Why?

In this sense, I think poverty can mean more than a few pennies in the bank. What about the wealth of one's own self-worth, based upon the satisfaction of knowing what one is, and liking what one sees in oneself?

The person without the ability to recognize life's challenges in the simple mundane tasks of life will:

1. Find it difficult to see and accept God in the ordinary aspects of day-to-day living. They confuse doing and being, forgetting who God wants them to be.
2. When the external pressure is not pushing, they find that there is no motivation for personal growth, making it easy to become discouraged.
3. In seeking to fill the void, have a strong tendency to turn to other extremes, such as: too much introspection, yoga, transcendentalism, the occult.

This brings us to the question: How does society seek to deal with the problem?

It is predicted that within the next few years, there will be one of the greatest psychic revolutions in the history of the world. Jerry Rubin, the well-known radicalist of the 60s, when asked in a television interview about what he foresaw for the future, stated the following: There will be a great change from the old patterns of demonstrations and open revolt to a pattern of self-awareness. He predicted trends toward transcendentalism that would sweep in to fill the void made by the generation of the past, and mentioned three things I thought interesting. They are:

1. A new emphasis will be placed upon the individual through yoga and meditation.
2. There will be a thrust toward health faddism.
3. There will be a blending of the self into one moment of ego strength, bringing the individual into a method of negating negativity.

Already we are seeing this take shape. Not only in the minds of those moving from radicalism; but, there is a growing tendency in our society toward the occult, and too much introspection. In the religious world, there are the super-spirituals who want to do basically the same thing, to dig into some remote mystical area to find answers.

I listen to these women, all of the time, who parade themselves in cloaks of great righteousness, going out on some "devil hunting" spree, taking great delight in their so-called ability to probe the personality of another. The truth is, they could easily be caught up themselves in little more than a cycle of spiritual faddism. Like vultures, they prey on susceptible victims. I cannot decide who is worse, the person who allows themselves to be trapped in this, or the person who victimizes them.

One thing I am sure: God is not a part of anything that brings confusion to the psyche. He is not a split personality and does not fragment the inner self! Wherever Christ went He touched people, making them better, bringing them into a total unison of the body, soul and spirit. The Bible itself tells us that

Christ grew with His life in perfect balance to his cultural surroundings, in growth and maturation, and in favor with God. Is this not proven in the Gospel of St. Luke?

> So Jesus grew both tall and wise, and was loved by God and man. Luke 2:52 Reach Out Edition

Now, the question of *how* does one find a balanced life? There are some simple guidelines listed below that might be helpful.

PLAN OF ACTION

1. Learn to look for God in the little things of life, in everything that touches you. If you examine those things carefully you will find, they, along with the bigger things, have the "fingerprint" of God upon them. If God's hand is upon them, they need nothing more for our acceptance.

2. Watch out for too much introspection. Someone has said for every one time we look inwardly, we need to take nine looks upward to keep in a good psychological/spiritual balance. Why? We know our own greatest weaknesses and tend to make more of them than God does. Therefore, we must learn to look at them through God's potential. If we are to examine ourselves in the light of the biblical command: 1 Corinthians 11:28, then we must use another, double lens.

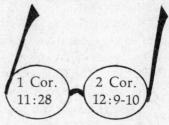

READ: Heb. 11:34 KJV

Our weakness must always be seen as God's channels for His strength to flow into us. There is no other way His strength can be made manifest to us until we recognize our own ineffectiveness.

3. By the recognition of our needs, and personality traits, we take the first step toward growth. Looking for some great "magic wand" of power to sweep it all away is little more than fantasy. So, when we talk about growth, we speak of something that is S-L-O-W. It doesn't come overnight. It is a gradual thing that is measurable, not by others, but by oneself in relation to where one is coming from.

A young Christian lady came to me not long ago, very disturbed over her supposed lack of spiritual growth. I had watched her over the past year and knew her to be a person of integrity. She had blossomed in her personality, and was a positive thinking individual who had overcome great obstacles during the previous months. Yet, she had retained a simple faith that we all had learned to admire. I was shocked when she came to me so troubled in spirit.

After some time of counseling, I asked her to look back on where she was the year before. We went through that year in a verbal imagery.

"How are you coping with those problems today?" I asked.

Then it dawned on her.

"Now, I see what you mean by not being able to see my own growth," she said. "The things that bothered me a year ago, are no longer a problem to me. I am moving into areas of growth, accepting new challenges I never knew I could do before."

Spiritual growth is much like the physical, it cannot be visualized. Most small children will tell you they are not growing and can only be convinced of the same as they are stood up to the wall and measured every few months. It is by comparison to where they were and where they are today that determines it.

Again, it is important to know that the fruit of the Spirit is a natural part of *"abiding;"* not the result of plucking oneself up over-and-over again, but of staying put while the inner self produces a plant of symmetry and balance.

Fruit of the Spirit is the direct result of abiding in the *vine . . . and . . . takes time.*

READ: Gal. 5-6, List the fruit of the Spirit.

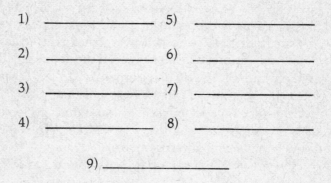

1) _____   5) _____

2) _____   6) _____

3) _____   7) _____

4) _____   8) _____

9) _____

STREAM OF MATERIALISM

Material priorities have a tendency to carry one into a "hot pursuit" of happiness; that person measures personal self-worth against the "have's and the have nots" of society. It is like searching for the illusive tomorrow that never comes, as if life consists only of the abundance of things.

4. When an overemphasis is placed on the material "care and feeding" of the physical body, a woman becomes primarily involved in:

What she wears . . .
Her latest wrinkle . . . and she
Refuses to accept her age!

This in turn effects her emotional state. She is crushed if she doesn't have all the *happiness* she thinks she deserves in life.

I believe one does not have to "go out" to find true happiness; that it is a child of the heart, given time and the right perspectives it will find you!

Real personality development comes from being able to put the legitimate needs of life on the right level of thinking; accepting God's added benefits when they come, and learning the joy of appreciating the todays.

True! There is no way to minimize the necessities of life. We all have needs basic to survival. Not all our needs are exactly the same. They may even vary in intensity or drive; none the less, they are actual, essential and existent. Perhaps it would help if you better understood what these needs are. Maslow, the psychologist, names these five as basic to human development:

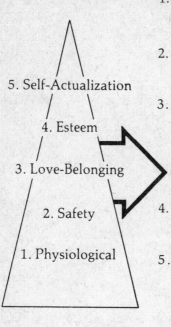

1. PHYSICAL - Food and the necessities for the physical well-being.

2. SAFETY - A sense of security for protection of self, family, home.

3. LOVE-BELONGING - The saying "everybody needs somebody" is true. We see this sense of belonging in lodges, clubs and fraternities.

4. ESTEEM - The desire for acceptance by one's peers.

5. SELF ACTUALIZATION - The need to be creative. To find one's own "niche" in the world.

According to Maslow's theory, it is impossible to find self-identity until the other basic needs are met. That is not the same way the Bible teaches it. In fact, it is the direct opposite to what Jesus said.

LOOKING AT SELF-NEEDS AS GOD SEES THEM . . .

UPSIDE

DOWN

. . . TO THE NATURAL WAY.

1. Being anxious for nothing
   Matt. 6:25-34
2. Security of believer
   Ps. 91
3. Self-love automatic in "Golden Rule"
   Luke 6:31
4. Self-worth linked with Christ
   Gal. 2:20
5. Linked to expendability with a purpose
   Matt: 16-25
6. . . .Christ reverses that principle and begins here

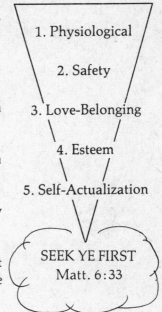

1. Physiological
2. Safety
3. Love-Belonging
4. Esteem
5. Self-Actualization

SEEK YE FIRST
Matt. 6:33

READ: Phil. 4:19

Write your need _____
Put the word "God" over it.

"MY GOD SHALL SUPPLY ALL YOUR NEED ACCORDING TO HIS RICHES IN GLORY." Phil. 4:19 KJV

Needs become a challenge based on the abundance of God's supply.

1. It is an unending, inexhaustible *resource*;
2. A never-failing *source*;

READ: Ps. 37:25, Lam. 3:22, Luke 16:17

   3. An always present *help*.

READ: Ps. 46:1

6

What are the
Effects of Extremism?

The woman herself, and she alone, determines the *effect* society is having upon her. (*Effect* is the direct result of a cause, trend, or existent situation.) Whether it is a subtle thing, or something we "fall-head-into," there has to be a reasonable cause to produce an effect.

Women, even Christian ones, are not immune to the resulting effects of misplaced value systems. Too many of us seem to evade the real cause and are stunned when we crash into the wall of harsh reality.

This is especially true in relation to an attitude of *comparative/competitiveness*: that terrible feeling of inadequacy which drives the woman to always be trying to prove her self-worth (to herself and others). She hides behind a self-martyr role, "work horse" image, always working a little harder for acceptance. Her inferiority sometimes takes on an "aire of superiority." What about this competitive syndrome, and how does it develop?

It is a slow, but subtle thing, affected by the

process of one's negative thinking. A woman looks at herself—does not like what she sees—compares herself to another, and the first step toward internalized rejection is begun.

This method of comparison is totally unfair!

Remember, no one has done anything so well that someone else did not learn to do it better. Records are made to be broken in every field, sports, business, and otherwise. Self-acceptance must not be based on these comparisons of so-called superiority. Talent is great, but it does not make one's character. A gorgeous face and figure is to be desired; however, that in itself does not make a beautiful woman. Yet, we are so guilty of building a life-style based on these things.

If I were to measure myself by you, I am sure to find many areas lacking in my life. This starts me on what I call the *"descent of personality."* My first step is *self-rejection*. I cannot self-reject without being angry with God for having cheated me out of so much, giving such large quantities to others. In so doing, my so-called weaknesses begin to loom out of proportion.

God-rejection blocks out the ability to find one's self. Doubt becomes a child of the heart. To say: you have *nothing* is to look up into the face of God and say, "God you cheated me—you gave something to everyone else but nothing to me." By so doing, all responsibility for failure, and lack of motivation, is transferred over to God. He becomes the *"scapegoat"* upon which you throw all of your inadequacies. When you become so wrapped in a sense of *false humility* that you cannot recognize the ability of God to work in you . . . through you . . . and for you, there is internal war!

The question then looms bigger and bigger: "Can God use me?"

Of course He can!

Is it unbelievable to think the God who knows us best does not LOVE US MOST? But, your concept of Him will limit His ability to work in you. Tim LaHaye emphasizes this by saying: "Everyone has an image of himself, either good or bad, but whatever that self-image, it affects our behavior, attitudes, productivity, and ultimate success in life." [4]

A few years ago, I was asked to teach a junior boys' Sunday School class in the absence of their teacher. Not having been forewarned, there was no time for preparation. In the room sat several kids that had been brought in off the streets. I was most anxious that they understand the concept of a kind, and loving heavenly Father. Beginning with a chalkboard, a pattern was quickly formed, as the children fed back to me, in one word, what they needed most from their earthly parent. After having gone through this "buzz" session with them, it was easy to relate their individual needs over to God their heavenly Father. Some time later, one of the mothers, whose son was in the class, came to me with this statement: "Ever since the lesson on one's personal relationship, and God's interest in the individual, our son has been changed. His whole personality is different! There was something about his discovery that God cared for him in such a personalized way, it seemed to give him an assurance of total acceptance."

Perhaps, if I had only one lesson to teach young

4. Tim LaHaye, *How to Win Over Depression* (Grand Rapids, Michigan, 1974) pp. 137-138.

people, it would be in this area: the importance of learning "who they are," and helping them move into an area of uninhibited living. Why?

Because when one fails to accept oneself in this child/father relationship, a barrier is set up toward others. This causes them to feel less than the other person by comparison, and there seems to be one thing left to do—COMPETE for equal acceptance! To pursue another avenue in which one can excel. That is not an abnormal reaction; yet, when it happens the person can literally run himself to death . . .doing. . . going.

So, the natural tendency is to bring the other person down to our level. One very negative manner in which this is done is through *criticism*. After all, why would anyone be critical of another, if it were not in an area where the other excelled; or, because of having recognized the same weakness in ourselves, we don't like it in the other person. By criticizing another, we make ourselves believe it is not a part of us. Hoping to make ourselves look better!

Two women were sitting discussing this subject, one of whom had been the object of severe and unfair "loose-tongue martyrdom." The victim felt devastated and could not understand "why" the attack. The other person explained it by saying: "Don't you know, they resent you; not as a person, but because you are what they want to be and cannot?" She went a little further with her remarks by pointing out to the other that: "We seldom criticize people whom we feel are lesser than us." Not a bad observation is it?

Frustration, fatigue and anxiety are the fruit of this bitterness, a spirit of negativism that robs the soul and thwarts personal growth. Thus, they are the cultural by-product of a society built on competition.

We have all had to watch these areas of our lives. Everyone is susceptible to the weakness, even the dearest of God's wonderful saints (if there are living ones). For this reason I have included a PLAN OF ACTION for the brave souls who are willing to admit they could have a problem in this area—and you do have to be brave to admit it!

PLAN OF ACTION

Self-help for *"Brave Souls"*!

1. Do I have a problem in any one of these areas?
   a) If so, what is it?
   b) What is my clue?
   c) When did it begin?

2. Is my problem directed toward any one individual?
   a) If so, to whom?
   b) Has it been a gradual thing?
   c) How long? (Try to pinpoint the reason, time, person.)

3. Do I want God's help? Really?
   a) Am I willing to apply the Scriptures as listed on the Descent of Personality Chart (page 60)?
   b) Will there be a conscious effort on my part to establish a right spirit between God, myself and others?

A Prayer for the "STRUGGLING SAINT"

Lord, teach me honesty. Help me that I will not hide behind coverings of my own "hang-ups," by spiritualizing them. I know you see me as I really am.

Give me the grace to accept personal responsibility for what I am, without laying blame, or transferring it over to you by saying: "God, you made me like this."

Thank you, Father, for showing me this area of weakness in my life. I will attempt to rise above it from this day forward, knowing "I can do all things through Christ which strengtheneth me."

P.S. Forgive me, Lord, for the times I goof up. I know I'm gonna!

Descent of Personality

1. COMPARISON

a) Self-Reject
b) God-Reject
c) Reject Others

2. COMPETE

a) Work Syndrome
b) Restless Spirit
c) Critical Attitudes

3. FRUSTRATION

a) Anxiety
b) Physical Exhaustion
c) Illness-Discouragement

4. DEPRESSION

a) Neurosis
b) Mental Disorders

1. TO COMPARE myself with another is totally unfair. Why?
   a) I know my weaknesses.
   b) I do not know yours.
   c) I am measuring my weaknesses against your strengths, blaming God for "cheating me!"

2. COMPETITION is not a part of God's plan.
   a) If I can't compare with you in one area of life, I will try to outdo you in another.

   b) Always joining, going, without the ability to have a *quiet* spirit before God.

   c) Tear you down to my level.

3. FRUSTRATIONS.
   a) No one can be happy with themselves, when they are resentful inside.
   b) The physical body cannot handle the unresolved guilt.
   c) Physical disorders resulting from stress, leading to discouragement are numerous (intestinal, heart, etc.).

4. DEPRESSION.
   a) Neurosis and inability to cope with life situations.
   b) Mental disorders followed by symptoms of a split personality.

WEARINESS VS. REST

These are days of much weariness. We can feel it in

our bones. It seems to be everywhere.

I've watched that "Geritol" commercial when the vibrantly-alive, charming female snuggles up to her husband and gets a "smack" on the cheek. Suddenly, I am made to feel my weariness is nothing more than "tired blood." That's it! That's my problem, I just need another vitamin, or—It seems easier to think that, rather than admit I might be having a spiritual difficulty in knowing when to say no to the demands of life.

Everytime my husband assumes a different pastorate, along with each mile of the moving van, there is a trail of new vows. I promise, with "Girl Scout's honor," I will never get so involved again. "Things are going to be different this time," I say.

Well! You guessed it. Soon my consuming desire for acceptance by this parish has driven me right back to where I was before. Then, "whammo," God has to remind me of *Who He is.*

Do you know, it is sometimes hard to accept that? Why?

Is it because we do not understand how physical fatigue affects our spirit life? I think we would be more cautious about overtaxing our bodies, in the disguise of spirituality, if we really knew.

Look at that "thundering" prophet Elijah, in 1 Kings 19:4-7. He sat under a juniper tree and begged God to kill him. "Just let me die," he said. Now, you and I both know, he didn't really want to die, out there alone, with no one to give his "eulogy." (After all, had he not done great things for which he deserved credit?) The man was just tired, just plain fatigued, and it would have been easier to have lain down—and stayed down.

The devil attacked Jesus on the Mount of

Temptation at the time of our Lord's greatest physical weariness. You notice Satan waited until the forty day fast was over, knowing that it would be the time when the Master would be most humanly vulnerable. You, too, if you stop to think, will discover that most of your discouragements have come in times of great physical exhaustion.

A friend called me one day to ask for prayer. I had no sooner answered the phone until I became aware that something was wrong with her. Her usual cheerful banter was gone. I could hear her sniffling on the other end of the line. After a few words of exchanged greetings, she poured her heart out to me.

"Will you pray with me?" she asked. "I don't believe God loves me anymore. I cannot feel Him and I never seem to get my prayers answered," she kept saying.

I listened to her, knowing something of the existing circumstance of her life. A close member of her family had been involved in a "freak" accident, leaving the relative as little more than a living vegetable. My friend had tried to assist in the care of the person, as well as care for her own growing family, and hold a full-time job. She had become weary, tired, mentally and physically fatigued. I knew that!

When she had finished speaking, it was evident that the thing bothering her most was her feeling of total isolation from God (which is not an uncommon reaction). It took quite some time to convince her that her problem was not a spiritual one at all; it was, primarily, a physical one. (In fact, she was so weary I doubt that she would have recognized God, had she met Him in the middle of the street.) After much reassurance that her problems had absolutely nothing to do with her God relationship, she began to think much more clearly.

Within a matter of days I happened onto the girl at a public meeting. It was most obvious something good had happened to her. She ran to me quickly and, with a big sigh of relief said, "What a thrill it was for me to understand the real source of my problem. God had been there with me all the time, I was just *too tired to recognize him!*"

Her frustrations were obvious ones. Ours are not always that easily observed; the reason being, most of our energy-stealers are subtle things that drain us gradually, making us weary and fatigued.

Listed below are five areas we need to guard carefully, since they represent times of great vulnerability.

1. When our spiritual resources have been depleted from neglect of the inner soul.
2. When our psychological ego has been tried to the point of weariness.
3. When our emotions are weary—and depleted—from a continued strain of pressing involvements.
4. When the physical body is down from illness.
5. When we have suffered from great losses, by disappointment, death, change.

This brings us to the question, "How do I cope with weariness?"

These are times when we must carefully watch ourselves, remembering the psychological effect is closely linked to the physical. We may even need to take another look at personal priorities by asking ourselves a series of questions, such as:

1. Do I have realistic goals? Are the goals I have set for myself within reason, or am I going right on "hammering away" at them, knowing full well they are dreams of idealism? If so, you are still dredging up the past of "what might have been," blocking out the potential of "what could be." And . . . you may be wondering why you are not productive, why you feel you cannot be used of God. The feeling is not tangible; it's just something that is there sapping at your strength. One great cause of depression is a result of this very thing. Look at how it works—

Self-inflicted Discouragement

CAUSE	EFFECT	ANSWER
Unreached goals	Ego-pride won't let you admit it.	Self-denial is the first step to growth. Matt. 16:24
Too much introspection	Self belittling putting limits on God.	2 Cor. 12:9
Unwillingness to face it	Blame others	Heb. 4:15

2. Do I have unresolved guilt? Do I feel fresh and clean from having asked forgiveness for a broken fellowship with God and others?
3. Do I observe the biblical pattern of rest and change for one day a week?
4. Am I profitably occupied with the needs of others, thus avoiding tiresome boredom.
5. Do I understand God's promises to those who are weary? Have I learned to let God talk to me through day-to-day living?

God's Word speaks to us very directly today! I'd like to suggest that you memorize this text, Isa. 40:28-31. Frank Hiller, who was a major league baseball pitcher a number of years ago, was pitching a game on a hot afternoon. The temperature was over 100. Suddenly he sagged with weariness out there on the mound and wondered how he could go through with it. Then, remembering Isa. 40:31, he repeated to himself: "But they that wait upon the Lord shall renew their strength. They shall mount up with wings like eagles; they shall run and not be weary; they shall walk and not faint" (TLB). Later he related that just by repeating these words new strength came to him. He finished the game with energy to spare!

PLAN OF ACTION

Restful/Quiet Spirit for "TIRED SAINTS!"

1. We are told to *study* to have a quiet spirit. 1 Thess. 4:11
2. It is called an *ornament* to you. 1 Pet. 3:4
3. Better than a houseful of *riches*. Prov. 17:1; Eccl. 4:6

How?

a) *Confidence* and *quietness* come from resting in God who brings *strength*. Isa. 30:15
b) Result of *listening* to what God says about you. Prov. 1:33
c) Direct reward of *righteous* living. Isa. 32:17
d) To be *cultivated* in the church. 1 Cor. 14:33; 2 Cor. 13:11; Phil. 4:2; Eph. 4:3

RECOMMENDED READING FOR "BUSY SAINTS":

Carlson, Dwight L. *Run and Not Be Weary*. Old

Tappan, New Jersey: Fleming H. Revell Co., 1974.
Lee, Earl G. *Recycled for Living*. Glendale, California: Regal Books, Division of G/S Publications, 1973.

FURTHER SCRIPTURAL STUDIES:

Isa. 53:5
Acts 10:36
Rom. 5:1
Eph. 2:14
Col. 1:20

FEAR VS. TRUST

When I was a child, my father's farmland joined the county cemetery. The burial grounds lay just up the hill from our house. In order to use the road across country, it was necessary to pass through a small ravine before topping the hill between our house and the cemetery. I can remember the dreaded walk around evening time when the tombstones cast their eerie shadows through the night. We children would brace ourselves against the lurking pranksters who delighted in hiding themselves in the bushes and jumping out at us. Our self-defense was to draw in a deep breath and run—just as fast as we could—not knowing we were being frightened by our own meaningless shadows most of the time.

How foolish it all seems to me now!

Yet, those experiences are not at all unlike many of life's situations. Is it not true, we spend much of our energies running from the imaginary illusions of fear during a lifetime?

I am afraid too many of us have done little more

than that! There is the constant running from something that does not exist—or never shall—and the heated "sprint," antagonized by fear. It is like a barking dog on our heels; our spiritual adrenalin seems to run on nothing more than fear.

Somehow, I cannot accept this as God's pattern for creative spiritual living. Franklin D. Roosevelt once said: "We have nothing to fear but fear itself."

That may be true! We all know, we cannot have both fear and trust at the same time. The minute one comes in the front door the other goes out the back.

Most of us have some *"thing"* that could give us a good case of the *"fears."*

In fact, I think we live in a fear/worry-oriented society!

Lately, so many women have been coming to me with this problem, I thought it might be good to find out what the general public fears most. My information has no scientific value, but it did prove to be interesting to me!

After a few days of listening to news releases and reading magazines, I jotted down some of the things I was being told to fear. They went something like this:

I was to have fear of . . .

1. An energy power shortage.
   (I turned off my electric blanket to save electricity, started riding my bicycle to save gasoline . . . but ran out of MY energy a few short blocks away.)
2. The earth going into an ice age.
   (I won't be around anyway, so no need to worry about that.)

3. The whole ecological balance being thrown off. Spray can chemicals are damaging the ionosphere.

   (God forbid, that I should do that! I rushed right out and bought the kind of hair spray that "squirts" with a pump, and comes out in "globs" all over; at least I don't feel guilty every time I comb my hair now!)

4. A loss of military power.

   (Can do nothing about that except vote for a politician who will take care of it . . . and the Lord only knows who that would be.)

5. A major earthquake throwing me right into the ocean.

   (I don't swim very well, so, I found a Scripture to help me with that one.)

   > Therefore, will not we fear, though the earth be removed, and though the mountains be carried into the midst of the sea. Ps. 46:2 KJV

   > "God is our refuge . . ." Ps. 46:1 KJV

6. Overpopulation of the earth.

   (Wow! My hysterectomy pulled me out of that one.)

7. Food preservatives.

   (I started to call my daughter long distance to make sure she was listening to the telecast. After all, I didn't want her poisoning my grandchildren. A "shocker" hit, about the time I went to pick up the phone:

   "There are over 4,000 additives in our foods," the man said.

I'll never drink another of those carbonated drinks, it's juices for me, I thought out loud to myself.

Then the anchor man inquired, "How many of you know that your packaged mix contains a preservative?"

That blew my scarf right off my head. "I thought the astronauts had taken it on their space flight . . . now . . . they had gone and polluted the moon!" I said.)

That is to say nothing of the commercials that seem to be designed to "scare me to death." Like the one with a house burning down, reminding me it could be mine; another, showing a grieving widow with small children and a too-small insurance policy. You probably have a few of your own that could be added here. Every woman has her own set of "Panic Mania." That little something she secretly fears.

When all of these things are happening around you, where do you go for help?

First, understand that these problems may be both real and unreal.

> FEARS:
> 40% never occur
> 30% are past and can't be changed
> 12% needless - about health
> 10% petty miscellaneous
> 8% legitimate

Earl Nightengale, a researcher discovered the formula above. If what he says is true, I have to cope with only eight percent of my fears; four percent of which are something I can help, and the other four percent I can do nothing about. That leaves me with a minimum of fears to begin to tackle. I must, then, begin to work on some method for resolving those I can do something about; the others are rolled over onto God. (They are too big for me to handle, anyway!)

Secondly, my own *fears* are to become the challenge for *"fear's defeat."* You might like to put your own ideas in here.

PLAN OF ACTION

Self-help for God's "FEARFUL SAINTS."

1. Deliver your *fears* to Calvary, knowing God does not give a *"fear spirit."* 1 John 4:18; 2 Tim. 1:7
2. Accept God's work as the final authority, believe in His keeping power. Isa. 41:10
3. Listen to what God says with expectancy . . . for He will speak *peace* unto His people. Ps. 85:8
4. Stay away from fear-oriented people.
5. Get with it and do what you can! If your heart is overwhelmed, then do what the person did in Ps. 61:2

He prayed:

> When my heart is overwhelmed and fainting lead me to the rock that is higher than I. Yes . . . a rock that is too high for me.
>
> For thou has been a shelter in the time of storm . . . (Amplified)

Further help for the "FEARING ONES."

1. List your fears and label them.

   _____   _____   _____
   already past   needless   petty

   _____
   real

2. Take the real ones; divide them into half.

   can help: can't help:
   _____   _____
   _____   _____
   _____   _____

3. Put the ones you can help on a sheet of paper;
   itemize them.

   a) Ask God to help you accept them.
   b) Offer the entire list to God as a challenge unto
      Him, to work for you.
   c) Burn up the list as a step of faith.

4. Begin to work on those fears you can do
   something about.

   a) Ask God for strength.
   b) Concentrate on a method.
   c) Keep working on them, even when you are
      afraid.

Prayer for a "FRIGHTFULLY SCARED SAINT:"

   Lord, these are the things I can do absolutely
nothing about. You really have some problems

here, they are big ones! I give them all to you, knowing "nothing is too hard for you." (See Gen. 18:14.)

About these things I can help: Lord, give me a spirit of determination as I set out to conquer them. I know there will be times when it would be easier to avoid them, than to face up to them; unless you help me, I cannot do it.

I go, in the promise of your help.

P.S. Oops, Lord, help me quickly, 'cause I'm already scared!

Unit II

Who Do You Want To Be?

7

Have You Discovered the Real You?

> What other people think of you is not nearly so important as what you think of yourself.
>
> Maxwell Maltz

The growing woman should seek to know herself in terms of personal acceptance. She should be able to reach outward and upward, as she looks inwardly. She alone determines the effect society is going to have upon her.

To look inwardly is not enough. Too much introspection can prove to be devastating! One has a tendency to overemphasize one's own weaknesses without recognizing the personal strengths.

Think with me, as we take a practical approach to the age-old question of "Who am I?" in terms of personality, likes and dislikes. For this reason I have chosen three biblical women, Mary, Martha, and Dorcas, as examples with whom you may be able to identify. You will discover you may have traits of all three of these. That is good! However, problems will develop when one characteristic becomes predominant throwing the total self out of balance with other areas of one's life.

Let's begin with Mary . . .

Mary, the Sensitive Woman
Luke 10:38-42

Who is Mary, the sensitive woman?

She is the one, who by her compassionate nature, and understanding heart, draws people to her like a "hummingbird looking for sugar." At the same time, this very kind, loving individual is a number one target for the "guilt syndrome" pattern.

Why is this?

Because the sensitive woman is a giver by instinct, she is also most vulnerable to guilt. It is for that reason, she should hang out a *"No Trespassing"* sign over her psychological ego. The menacing ghost of self-condemnation will intrude itself upon her if she is not careful. It will stalk her, using her as a prey to frustration, fatigue, and spiritual terror; unless, she becomes aware of its potential in her life.

The qualities of the sensitive woman's strengths are also her very weakest points. She has a tendency, while helping someone with their problems, to absorb them into herself like a "giant sponge." Her life then is lived, consciously or unconsciously, through the struggles of others. In her eyes, to take out time for her self needs would be almost selfish. As a result of this attitude, she may easily become the martyr for someone she loves—and, do it willingly. Nothing is too good for those she serves.

What a tremendous person!

But wait a minute! What about her susceptibility to those who would use her? Since it is easier for her to say yes than no, she may find herself involved in more projects than she can possibly get done. If she is married to a husband who is a "getter," and she is a "giver," there will be an endless cycle of continued giving until something breaks. Usually, it is her health!

While she is giving, she may also have some very strong feelings of pent-up emotions against those persons she is doing the most for. There are feelings of being taken for granted, or of being imposed upon, that will begin to surface sooner or later.

This is where the guilt comes in. Two things begin to occur simultaneously: One, on the part of the woman herself; the other, on the part of the people around her. They have come to expect an established behavioral pattern. Their expectations are based upon her past actions. Since she has always put the feelings of others first, they have grown to accept it. Any deviation from the "grooved" procedure, hits them like a "shock wave." The reactions coming from them can be similar to that of a "baby earthquake." The small ripple of personal change that started with one individual, has now grown into a tidal wave. It has begun to hit against the shores of "home sweet home." After all, the serene—or not-too-serene— pattern to which the family has grown accustomed is now being threatened. The very one who created that environment is now taking it away from them. That can be disturbing to those persons touched by it, whether it is a husband, wife, or whomever. Change can be a painful thing!

While those around may be suffering, there is the individual who is trying to break loose, who also suffers. That sensitive woman, who has dared try and move out, becomes a victim of her own self. She remains that same sensitive woman she was before she started, only now she is struggling with another problem: feelings of guilt! Guilt that is being thrust upon her by the reaction of her peers—those who feel she has walked out on them.

So, the woman who begins to break from her old habits of behavior will need to have a good self-understanding. She needs a full recognition of her individual self-worth before God. A verbal assertion of "things are going to be different around here" is just not enough. There must be positive goals toward which she is working. Change just for the sake of change is never good!

There must be a willingness to admit the hard, cold facts of life and the strength to brace up to the problems of misunderstood responses. The earlier she can face up to these facts, the better off she will be.

The woman who can accept those responses as adjustments, rather than a personal affront, will be able to move in the process of change much easier than someone who does not.

This is where balance comes in! The sensitive person who can bring herself into an even "keel" early in life is most fortunate. If she does not, she may begin to find it difficult to understand the attitude of those around her; why they are not as responsive to her needs as she is to theirs; or why others cannot share with her as willingly as she with them.

She asks: "After all, when I enjoy remembering others (for Marys are usually very thoughtful), why don't my friends and family reciprocate in the same way?"

And, because they do not respond to her needs as quickly, and liberally, she might be tempted to suffer quietly, nursing her wounds beneath a facade of temporary silence. (I say temporary, because the "weeds of resentment" never lie dormant long.) While resentment and bitterness may be buried, hidden from view, they never die!

It is amazing how quickly they show their ugly heads. Just as I have watched a tiny plant as it pushed its way from beneath a concrete slab, even so, I have seen the seedlings of hate and hostility explode, destroying people physically, emotionally, and spiritually.

One day, I went to call on a young lady in my husband's parish. When I arrived at her home, I found the shades drawn and her doors tightly locked. In fact, she hesitated before permitting me to enter. Her hair was unkempt, and her eyes were swollen, almost shut, from long hours of crying.

The home was in almost "apple pie" order, which reinforced the image of her "ideal motherhood" role. Those who knew her, knew there was no other lady in the neighborhood who could entertain with greater poise than she. Whatever she did was done and given her very best. This included teaching a Sunday School class, working a bus route, and numerous school activities. Somewhere in between, she was finding the time to raise three active boys.

Finding her in this kind of mental attitude was disturbing to me. She had always seemed to be on top of any situation. This day things were different! So, I listened as she shared, then we prayed, then we shared again. Finally, after hours of talking, the real problem surfaced.

She said: "I have lived in this house for years. All of my neighbors know I am a Christian. They seem to like me, but they impose upon me."

She named off her list: "One lady comes each week to have her hair set, another brings her children by for me to baby-sit them. The church is asking me to give more time to teaching. Why doesn't someone do something to help me occasionally? Do they think I would not enjoy a lovely meal in their home? Why am I always the one who does all of the entertaining?"

She was down—very down—not understanding what was happening inside. There was a feeling of strong desire for acceptance; a fear of rejection if she refused to do all the things she had been doing. Indeed she was one of the dearest young mothers one would hope to meet. However, her family and friends had begun to take her for granted. They were totally oblivious to her needs. She could not understand that!

But, when I suggested she withdraw from some of her many interests, it was almost too much for her to grasp. She felt as if she would be giving something less than her best to God and others. It took some time before convincing her that she could reorient her life into proper priorities and become an even more effective Christian.

What she had never come to realize was: One can perform outwardly while inwardly there is an endless cycle of self guilt, displaced aggression, and transferred blame. And, sometimes the tendency is to do more and more to prove ones self-worth. In this case, here was a young sensitive mother, who was taking on more than any one person could possibly do. She was breaking down physically while carrying the whole spiritual load of her home and family. (Her husband was not a Christian at the time.)

It might be interesting for you to know she did make some changes, and her husband became a Christian within a few months. The sad thing is, her spirit had become deeply wounded. Because of that, she had lost confidence in people, and was discouraged in her God relationship.

That is where the real danger is!

It is most difficult for a wounded spirit to keep a good perspective toward God. Strong sensitivities are always followed by feelings of deep emotional needs. There is the need for approval, a craving for affection and reassurance of acceptance. These are all needs common to the psychological framework of the sensitive woman.

I know it is sometimes hard to be honest about these feelings. It may be easier to just fence them off and pretend they do not exist. However, it is not until we have faced up to them and are honest with God that help really comes.

The question is: "Where does one begin?" How does the woman who suddenly becomes aware of this need make her break from the old patterns? Below are 10 basic steps that give some suggested guidelines toward self-fulfillment in the sensitive, Mary, personality.

1. You must be prepared to take the repercussion from those around you, who may not understand the change within you.
2. Make any change slowly, deliberately, handling each problem as the need arises. Never plunge yourself into some drastic declaration for self-fulfillment.
3. Communicate your feelings, whatever they are, expressing your personal desires in a spirit of love. DO NOT talk about your feelings of need if your emotions are not under control.
4. Be patient! Try and understand that it will take time on the part of others around you. Compliment the efforts of your spouse and others, give them credit for trying. They may want to understand more than you think.
5. DON'T expect too much too soon.
6. Be firm and have a goal you are reaching toward.
7. Become involved in something you yourself like to do. Avoid the temptation to feel guilty taking a few minutes each day for yourself.
8. Maintain a good balance. Be careful you don't threaten to walk out on the whole project.
9. Learn from experience. Ask others for help . . . and accept it.
10. Build the inner self through a good faith-building book.

TAKE ONE DAY AT A TIME AND DO NOT PANIC WHEN YOU GOOF!

Eccl. 3:22   There is nothing better than that a
              woman should rejoice in her own works
              for that is her portion. KJV-Paraphrased

1 Sam. 30:6 David encouraged himself in the LORD!
            KJV

Martha, the Perfectionist
Luke 10:38-42

The perfectionist is that idealist whose far-reaching goals keep her going in a precision-like pattern. Each detail of her carefully planned life is handled with such meticulous fervor, she often burns herself out with the "bonfire of trivia." She dares do nothing, unless it is done to perfection, and demands no less from others. She tends to live in a "straight jacket" of schedules!

This kind of personality will often become a slave to the temporal things of life. Martha must have been a woman of this temperament. However, I must admit, I have a great deal of appreciation for her. I am sure the Lord liked her too. If he scolded her, it was not because she wanted a clean house. Rather, because she had a cumbersome spirit! She was weighted down with a desire for perfectionism. The menu of the evening was "Martha's Delight," a gourmet treat for the Master. She was caught up in the nonessentials, while in her presence sat the *perfect Redeemer.*

How often we get caught in this yoke of bondage, cumbered, loaded down with doing the lesser important task. At the same time, we are missing the joys of watching our children grow up, growing up with them—and letting the yard grow up a little bit with all of us. The wife who is too busy to go when her husband invites her, cannot leave the dishes to enjoy her guests, and fights dust as if it were an "evil spirit," is headed for physical chaos.

In the very early part of my husband's ministry, we were given our first assignment. It was a small church in a little town in Southern California. The old parsonage was adjacent to the sanctuary, with only a driveway in between. Our furniture consisted of a potpourri of junk. We had a dining room table with one leg broken, a kitchen cupboard without doors, and enough cockroaches to frighten the cats away. I never worried much about the house burning. I always felt the cockroaches would put it out.

We have always had lots of company; and in spite of the falling table leg, the unmatched curtains, and the old rose couch, there was a homey atmosphere in the manse.

Everything was moving along nicely until one day my husband announced the soon arrival of a guest speaker. He was an official of our church denomination, and was bringing his wife to be overnight guests in our home. What a weekend it was!

My desire for perfection drove me into an immediate "frenzy." Every window in that house was cleaned that week. Every curtain was laundered. The floors of each room were paste waxed and hand buffed. They shone like glass. The quilts were run through the Maytag wringer washer. Everything was "spic and span" in readiness for my distinguished guests.

Everything but me—I was pooped! On Saturday before their arrival, my husband consented to do the grocery shopping. He decided, arbitrarily, to change my menu from roast beef to meat loaf. (That has always been, and still is, his favorite Sunday dinner.) When he returned home from the grocery store with two pounds of pork sausage, and two pounds of hamburger, I took it in good stride—with clinched teeth.

All went well until Sunday morning. (The speaker had spent the night with us, the evening before.) I rose early to prepare the dinner meal and serve breakfast. We were all settled around the table with the shakey leg. (Actually, we had a pretty good system worked out for keeping the leg on the table. My husband, who is a tall man, would sit at the end keeping one knee anchored solidly beneath the table top, in case the table slipped during the meal.)

There was a smug feeling of satisfaction that swept over me at the breakfast table. Everything seemed well under control. My husband, Claude, offered grace in his usual "preacher's voice." He thanked God for the provisions of the day. Then he told Him how welcome the visiting family was. It was as if he hoped they were listening in on his prayers. I sat there with my fingers crossed, praying a different kind of prayer. I was half grateful for my guests, half ungrateful. I knew the Lord understood me, though, and I hoped He would not hold it against me.

It was not until someone passed the sausage that I discovered what I had done. In my frenzied rush, the hamburger had been cooked for breakfast, and I had made a meat loaf of the sausage. We managed to laugh through the breakfast ordeal. I quickly salvaged the dinner loaf, and with all the outward "piety of a saint," began preparing the children for worship.

Our children, Deanna and Jan, were three and five at the time. I took great care in seeing that they were starched and ruffled to perfection. The ritual began early for them. Their baths were given on Saturday night, and their hair was shampooed and curled. The combing had to be done on Sunday morning. Part of getting them ready for church, was to take a bottle of wave set (the slick kind used for finger setting) and comb it through the hair to hold it neatly in place.

That morning, as I dipped the comb into the full bottle of wave set, intending to gently remove the excess from the comb, I knocked the bottle onto the bathroom floor. There lay the "gooey" mess at my feet. Have you ever tried mopping up wave set? The sensation is unbelievable.

Well, I managed to get through morning worship hours with a reasonable amount of serenity. However, tranquility did not last long. When I returned to the parsonage, I discovered one of the "little church demons" had beaten me there. My yeast rolls had been left on the kitchen table for rising. When I peeked in, I saw a pan full of something that looked like twelve white-dimpled rocks. The little "Pillsbury" man had been deflated. Some child had come through the house and punched each roll.

It was then I decided how much I had missed. Instead of enjoying the pleasure of my guests, I had been caught up in the cumbersome yoke of getting everything in perfect order. It was as if their acceptance of me depended upon the cleanliness of my home. I missed the pleasure of discovering a new friend! It would have been so much better had I reserved some of my strength for the enjoyment of their lovely company; or, getting to know them as persons.

What about you? This has not come easy for me; but, I am still working on it. These are some of the areas in which I am learning, by:

1. Stopping periodically and reevaluating my priorities, I am able to keep in a better balance.

2. Listening for cues from my husband that indicate his feelings when the atmosphere in the home is getting a little too stuffy.

3. Making a deliberate effort to make my guests feel welcome in my home, without running behind them picking up after them.

4. Stopping to analyze where my time is being spent—doing what—in relation to time spent developing more meaningful human relationships.

5. Sitting at the table enjoying a conversation with my husband or friends without feeling I have to jump right up and clear the table.

6. Serving meals that are less formal, more relaxed, to cut down on the work load.

7. Serving my friends whatever I serve the family without making apologies about it.

8. Not apologizing to my guests who arrive early, or who decide to drop in unexpectedly, even if the work is not yet finished. To apologize makes the guest feel like an intruder.

9. Having simple meals planned ahead and in the deep-freeze, for days that are interrupted in schedule.

10. Making my own daily calendar flexible enough for change.

Dorcas
Acts 9:36-39

Dorcas, the compulsive runner, the gazelle, for that is exactly what her name means. One has only to look at the quick-footed animal to understand what this woman is like. We have a good profile of her in this scriptural setting:

> Now there was at Joppa a certain disciple named Tabitha, which by interpretation is called Dorcas: this woman was full of good works and almsdeeds which she did . . . and all the widows stood by him weeping, and shewing the coats and garments which Dorcas made, while she was with them. Acts 9:36, 39 KJV

Have you ever stood back and watched these women go? They seem to have an endless source of energy. The energetic outflow of their work seems easy, unspoiled by any physical limitations of strength. They are good at everything they touch, and they touch everything around them. Wherever they are, the Dorcas influence is keenly felt, as well as heard.

They are the kind of women who can join all the clubs, run an efficient household, participate in sports, and be chairperson of the Garden Club. They never seem to struggle with their figures, because the metabolism of the Dorcas keeps her in motion.

But . . . "woe be unto her and others" if she is caught in a situation where she cannot be a part of a vital and moving unit. She may have a tendency to get *something going* . . . just for the sake of *doing*. It is difficult for her to understand the difference in *"working with God and for Him."* She lives to work and works to live—and it is usually carried over into her spiritual relationship with God!

What a beautiful characteristic that can be! I am reminded of a quotation by John McAfee:

> "Work, thank God for it,
> The ardor, the urge, the delight of it.
> Work that springs from the hearts desire,
> Setting the heart and soul on fire."

This seems to be the motto of the woman we are discussing. But there is, or can be, a problem there! She may not be able to understand why those around her are unable to keep pace with her. Working circles around everyone else, and keeping a quiet spirit at the same time, is a hard thing to manage. The tendency is to expect others to do as much as we. It is impossible!

Why is it so?

The woman with whom you work, if you are a Dorcas, may by the very nature of the genes of her heredity be unable to function on the same spirited level as you. I know women who are up and combed, powdered and ready for the day by 8:00 a.m. Not me!

For years this was a real problem with me. I am a s-l-o-w mover in the mornings. Now, I don't mean I can't move when I have to. When my babies were small I tried rising early for my devotions. Do you know what I found myself doing? My head usually ended up drooping, with my hair hanging in the coffee cup. I tried this over and over again, until I went through the whole cycle of guilt. Condemnation was heaped upon me in every woman's Bible class I attended. There the chic little gal would stand, as she told her secret of mobility. The longer she talked the worse I felt. Until I discovered . . .

God didn't really care whether my quiet time of service to Him was at 6:00 *a.m.* or at 10:00, He was just interested that I follow Him to the best of my individual ability. Besides, when those "girls" were sacked out early, I was still up scrubbing floors, tending my family, and really at my best about 11:00 *p.m.* It may be God planned it that way, so He could hear *"praise"* ascending unto Himself all hours of the day and night. So, I decided to let the early risers take their shift early—as early as they liked. I would take mine at the later hour. Somehow I cannot feel that made me a lesser Christian.

Dorcas women are go-getters until they come to the place they cannot, by reason of illness or otherwise, do as they have always done. They seldom learn the secret of our Lord's words:

> Come ye yourselves apart into a desert
> place, and rest awhile. Mark 6:31 KJV

If they do stop the whirlpool of activities, they have a tendency to fall apart, mentally, physically and spiritually. The same drive is thwarted, leaving them dejected, psychologically low, and they become victims of defeat because their only ministry (supposedly) has been taken from them. This can, very easily, result in a lethargic attitude toward important opportunities of service in new and creative areas. They would rather do nothing than dare make a change. It is for this reason that I have suggested a *"Plan of action in the morning"* for the Dorcas personality.

PLAN OF ACTION

1. Lie down flat and prop your knees up with a large pillow.
2. Beginning with the toes, tense all the muscles of your feet. Then tense all the muscles, moving upward—to the knees and thighs, pelvis, stomach, chest, neck, arms, and fingers—until the entire body is taut.
3. Remain in that position, keeping the body tense, to the count of ten.
4. Slowly release the toes, feet, knees, thighs, stomach, arms, throat and head.
5. Remain in that relaxed position for two minutes. While lying there, mentally draw from the Bible your favorite Scripture verse. Recall it over and over in your mind.
6. Visualize the twenty-third Psalm. Silently meditate upon the words of the psalmist, while remaining in that same quiet and relaxed position.

   Ask yourself:

   "I am sheep of his pasture" . . . what does a spiritual shepherd provide for his sheep? Let your mental images of that Great Shepherd flow freely . . . visualize yourself as one of his sheep . . . try to remember some of the provisions He has given you in the past. Be grateful for them.
7. When you begin to feel tense or afraid, STOP! Turn your thought to the source of your strength.
8. Fix your heart on a principle of God's Word and make His promise a living vital part of your day's believing.

9. Accept anything that comes into the day as having been "first touched by the hands of the *Master*."
10. Begin each morning knowing . . .

"This is the day the Lord hath made!"

. . . THEN REJOICE AND BE GLAD IN IT.

On the next two pages you will find a profile test that may be helpful to you in better understanding *"who you are."* Have fun as you go a little further in the study!

Just remember, we all have a mixture of traits that are readily distinguishable from among all three of these. So, just check yourself for balance and see which one is predominately YOU. Are you a Mary, Martha, or a Dorcas?

SELF-DESCRIPTION TEST

Below are some statements that will help you to know about yourself. Fill in each blank with a word from the suggested list following each statement. For any blank, three in each statement, you may select any word from the list of twelve immediately below. An exact word to fit you may not be in the list, but select the words that seem to fit MOST CLOSELY the way you are.

1. Most of the time I feel _calm_ , _contented_ and _impetuous_ .

calm	relaxed	complacent
anxious	confident	reticent
cheerful	tense	energetic
contented	impetuous	self-conscious

2. When I study or work, I seem to be ___enthusiastic___
___precise___ and ___determined___.

efficient	sluggish	precise
enthusiastic	competitive	determined
reflective	leisurely	thoughtful
placid	meticulous	cooperative

3. Socially, I am ___tolerant___, ___considerate___
and _____.

outgoing	considerate	argumentative
affable	awkward	shy
tolerant	affected	talkative
gentle-tempered	soft-tempered	hot-tempered

4. I am rather ___warm___, ___introspective___
and ___serious___.

active	forgiving	sympathetic
warm	courageous	serious
domineering	suspicious	soft-hearted
introspective	cool	enterprising

5. Other people consider me rather ___optimistic___,
___sensitive___ and _____.

generous	optimistic	sensitive
adventurous	affectionate	kind
withdrawn	reckless	cautious
dominant	detached	dependent

6. Underline one word out of the three in each of the following lines which most closely describes the way you are.

a. assertive, relaxed, tense
b. hot-tempered, cool, warm
c. withdrawn, sociable, active
d. confident, tactful, kind
e. dependent, dominant, detached
f. enterprising, affable, anxious

KEY TO SELF-DESCRIPTION

MARTHA Luke 10:38-42	DORCAS Acts 9:36-39	MARY Luke 10:38-42
Affable	Active	Anxious
Affected	Adventurous	Awkward
Affectionate	Argumentative	Cautious
Calm	Assertive	Considerate
Complacent	Cheerful	Cool
Contented	Competitive	Detached
Cooperative	Confident	Gentle-tempered
Dependent	Courageous	Introspective
Forgiving	Determined	Meticulous
Generous	Dominant	Precise
Kind	Domineering	Reflective
Leisurely	Efficient	Reticent
Placid	Energetic	Self-conscious
Relaxed	Enterprising	Sensitive
Sluggish	Enthusiastic	Serious
Sociable	Hot-tempered	Shy
Soft-hearted	Impetuous	Suspicious
Soft-tempered	Optimistic	Tactful
Sympathetic	Outgoing	Tense
Tolerant	Reckless	Thoughtful
Warm	Talkative	Withdrawn

Key to self-description test: Count the number of
adjectives that you selected in each of the three

categories. For example, if your totals are 10-6-5, you have predominantly MARTHA traits. A 6-10-5 means you are high in DORCAS traits, etc.

Luke 10:38

1. What is meant by the word "cumbered?"
   Write the definition.
   Correlate it with Luke 21:34.
   Give the definition of the word "surfeiting."

2. Did you rate high/low in each category? Which?
   High _Martha_ Low _Dorcas_ Other _Mary_
   Explain what is meant, in Luke 10:42, by the phrase,
     "One thing is needful . . . ."

3. Do you see yourself in good balance with the traits illustrated by all three biblical women?

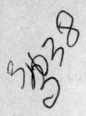

8

Can You Be the Person You Were Meant to Be?

Since women are expected to be everything everyone else wants them to be, they may feel themselves a failure if they are anything less!

I do not think today's woman is hung up on being "Sarah" or "Esther" or "Ruth" of the Bible! It's easy enough to see those women were human, by what the Bible reveals, though their virtuous characteristics are indeed worthwhile as a goal.

Instead, the twentieth century woman is having trouble trying to live up to her mama, his mama, or "His Majesty," the husband's expectations. The guilt can be strongly felt, when she finds she cannot be what she thought "she could be;" or, when she finds out she can't even be "what she wants to be."

Again, as we have discussed before, no one person can be all things to all people! However, it is important to have a sense of knowing *what the expectations of others* are and the demands they place upon you. At the same time, you dare not lose sight of what *you yourself want to be*. Notice also that these two images may not, in turn, harmonize with what you envision *God wants you to be*. That is the very thing that causes fragmentation of the personality!

When the three images become widely separated, and the gap keeps widening, you are in trouble! The inner self becomes divided, your self-identity is lost in a maze. You will find yourself vacillating back and forth, protecting the ego of your reputational character and the super-ego.

Every woman tires of being "out there somewhere" in a place where she cannot define her own role; everyone else is doing it for her, and she is unable to distinguish between the demands.

"Why won't people accept me for what I am?" is the question she asks herself (and we all *have*, at some time or other).

It is like the girl growing up, who is taught to do everything like her mother does it. When she marries she is expected to live up to the ideal of both "his and hers," (mothers, that is). Husbands think the new bride should be able to bake "apple pie" and make biscuits just like "his and her" mother. (Heaven forbid! Doesn't he know the minute the young wife did, she would blow the mother's ego right off their family tree?) Besides, any smart girl knows she should add another pinch of salt to the other woman's recipe, just to protect her own originality. No thinking person, young or old, wants to be a carbon copy of anyone else, no matter how much she might admire them.

The truth of the matter is: She certainly doesn't want to model her life after the person being set up as her example. Her cooking "thing" may be apple streudel and canapes, and she wants the pleasure of reserving that right for herself—without the feeling that she is being forced into doing what others have done, and fitting herself into the image of what they are.

I was made well aware of this years ago. Sue telephoned me for an appointment, which I arranged within a matter of days. She arrived, at the office, visibly embarrassed as if afraid to expose her problem. Finally, after a few moments of stammering she blurted it out:

"I am confused, terribly resentful, and hate life itself. All my life I have tried being what everyone else thought I ought to be. On the outside there is a facade covering the hostility of my inner hatred. I dislike every minute of playing the role of a model Christian. I am tired of defending the image others have set for me . . . and . . . I want to break loose. I am finding it most difficult to do because of fear of rejection by those who love me."

This lady had grown up in a small community and raised her family there. The city had a subculture all its own. To complicate the situation further, there was a strong cultural concept of traditional church negatives, within her environmental surroundings. Peers had made her believe that God's acceptance was dependent upon her living within their set of social norms. So, to please them she was conforming externally, but a "civil war" was raging inside. As a result of all this, Sue had begun to withdraw into a shell, feeling guilty before God, rejecting herself, and resenting those who had "caged her in their neat little traditional boxes of dos and don'ts."

How was Sue to deal with this problem?

1. She, in her willingness to discuss it had already taken the first, most important step.

2. Her ability to face up to the possibility of dis-
approval from those persons around her opened
up a new avenue of creativity to her.

3. By understanding who she was under God, as
an individual, the challenge of her new
environment was no longer a threat to her ego.

4. When her true identity was revealed and the
barriers broken down, she was free to pursue a
new dimension in creative living—and liked
what she was seeing in herself.

5. The recognition of God's acceptance moved her
into a harmonious blending of experience, interpersonal relationships, and self-appreciation.

Today, she is a very successful woman in her own
right.

Strange isn't it, that others seem to have a clear
picture of what we ought to be? Unfortunately, it is
sometimes most difficult to know the difference
between what God demands and what they expect!
So, we let them bind burdens upon us that are too
heavy for us to bear. Is this not what Jesus talked
about, concerning the Pharisees of his day?

. . . For you crush men beneath impossible
religious demands—demands that you
yourselves would never think of trying to
keep. Luke 11:46 Reach Out Edition

Those religious people in Jesus' day, were all bound
up in the letter of the law, cold icy legalism! They
were also the very persons who persecuted him most.
Their idea of a Messiah was not at all in harmony
with God's plan. "Be a breadwinner, help us throw
off our yoke of Roman bondage," they yelled at him.
Yet, the true success of Christ's ministry was in his
refusal to be pushed into their mold. He would not be

intimidated into being something different than what He was. He had decided that on the Mount of Temptation before his ministry ever began. (Which leads me to believe, we too need a time of settling the fact of what we know God wants for us in a personal way.) Christ had come for one purpose and one alone: To do the will of his heavenly Father! And, after only three-and-a-half years of earthly ministry, He was able in his dying hours to look up to God and say:

> I have finished the work which thou
> gavest me to do.   John 17:4 KJV

Need I remind you? All the lepers were not yet healed. The poor were still with them. He did not do all of the things the disciples had hoped He would do. Yet, Jesus had done *all God had given him to do*.

UNDERSTANDING THE DIFFERENCE!

READ: What was the motive of the Pharisees' actions? Matt. 23:4-7

To whom does one owe complete obedience? Matt. 23:10

DIFFERENCE:
God's conviction is
"free"-ing.
Others' accusations
"bind"-ing.
God's requirements
"love"-ing.
Others oriented in
"fear"-ing.

HOW DO THE THREE IMAGES FIT?

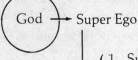

God → Super Ego

1. Super ego of our lives.
2. Conscience of right and wrong.
3. Concerns our soul needs.

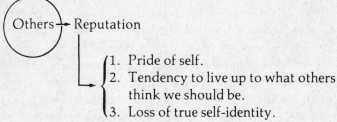

Others → Reputation

1. Pride of self.
2. Tendency to live up to what others think we should be.
3. Loss of true self-identity.

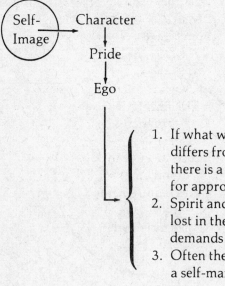

Self-Image → Character
↓
Pride
↓
Ego

1. If what we know we are, differs from our reputation, there is a constant struggle for approval, acceptance.
2. Spirit and personality is lost in the drive to meet demands.
3. Often the person becomes a self-martyr.

OTHERS AND THEIR IMPOSED GUILT

When other people's expectations are far removed from the image we have of ourselves three things happen: A resistance builds up against the person— or persons—applying the pressure; inner hostility becomes a part of our defense mechanism; and we seek methods to resolve the frustration.

Very early in my husband's ministry, I ran into a situation that clearly describes what I am speaking about. You will agree, that most people have a mental image of what a preacher's wife should be like. Right? They see her as a "saintly madonna" seated on the organ stool, surrounded by a "halo of effervescent smiles." Somehow by virtue of the person she is married to, she is expected to be a prima donna in the choir loft and much, much more. Well, I am none of those! I can't even say I am blessed with a lot of pulchritude (I think that means loveliness and beauty). Yet, I am one! (a minister's wife, that is).

For some people my lack of musical ability is a real problem. Like the so-called saint (I know she was one 'cause she looked so pious) who came stalking up to me. Her face was twisted as tightly as her straight-backed hair and the bun that rested on her arthritic neckline. She zeroed in on me with two penetrative eyes, and then started the steady stream of questioning:

"Honey, do you play the piano?"

"No, ma'am, I answered.

"What about singing, do you do that?" she inquired of me.

"I am sorry, I don't sing either."

After having reached the obvious conclusion that I was not qualified to be a wife to my husband, she turned and went into deep meditative thought. Finally, she put one spindly finger up to her mouth, and with a kind of hopeless gesture (as if the only possible thought she could come up with) said:

"Well, dear, perhaps you can pray!"

To this day I have not understood why she was so perplexed; unless, it was because I had completely destroyed the image of what she thought I ought to be (or, if she blamed me for having "messed up" my husband's life).

Anyway, there were two ways in which I could have responded. One in total rejection; the other, by determining my self-worth before God and refusing to accept imposed guilt for something I could not change.

This principle is true whether it is in the area of talents, role conflicts, traditional bindings, or whatever. I never discuss this in women's meetings without the question being raised, "How can I know what 'imposed guilt' is?"

It might help if we take a look at how traditional concepts take form; also, to understand that cultural "trappings" are most difficult to change and may introduce a "guilt syndrome" from others toward you. The chart below will give you an idea of what is meant by cultural norms.

SOCIOLOGICAL CHART

FADS   Result of someone doing something differently, that begins to "take" with one segment of society or a particular group within a unit, i.e., fashion, hair styles, clothing, is called a FAD.

TRENDS

When enough people begin doing the particular thing a TREND develops and spreads. The person who has a poor self-image will seek to conform, whether it conflicts with inner principles or not. The self-fulfilled individual does not move into fads as quickly. Other things are of more importance, external pressure is weighed by internal value systems.

MORES

Whatever the TREND is, it will soon become a part of the MORES, or customs by the majority as it eventually becomes socially acceptable.

This is where the twentieth century woman feels the "pull." She cannot, in some cases, accept the NORM as being in harmony with her personal conviction of principle. And she may choose not to conform, even if there is no conflict of spiritual values. Paul, in writing to the early church, sounded a kind of warning to today's woman. He said: "Don't copy the behavior and customs of this world, but be a new and different person with a fresh newness in all you do and think. Then you will learn from your own experience how His ways will really satisfy you." Rom. 12:2 TLB

TRADITION

Subcultures begin to form through small units—family, church, ethnic, and community groups. They adopt certain forms of trends and methods, as the only acceptable pattern for living. And in the case of religion, subcultures may take on traditional forms that have little or nothing to do with Jesus' teachings.

MORAL CODES

MORAL CODES are set up to enforce the tradition. In some church circles this can be based on external negatives of dos and don'ts.

LAWS

LAWS are made to demand obedience to a moral code, making it territorial or universal.

The very minute a woman begins to move away, or to question the rules set by traditionalism, she becomes most vulnerable to guilt being heaped upon her by her peers. (I should like to stop here and make one thing perfectly clear: I am not talking about biblical principles relating to those things clearly defined in Scripture. I speak of cultural norms, geographically that have absolutely nothing to do with one's relationship to the heavenly Father.)

So, let's take a look at ourselves in relation to this kind of guilt.

PLAN OF ACTION

1. Ask yourself, "Are other people forcing me into their personal image of conformity?" If so, in what way?
2. What is the source of the guilt? Is it because I disagree and am not willing to face up to them? Or, is it because I am unsure of my own principles regarding the matter?
3. Do I consider the traditional concept in perfect harmony with other biblical principles? Or, is it an area that has been imposed upon me by years of trying to conform?
4. Do I understand that traditionalism brings pressure and possible self-guilt if I move away from it?
5. Can I differentiate between God's demands and other people's?

SCRIPTURAL REINFORCEMENT:

Christ's indictment to the Pharisees. Matt. 23:1-12
The command not to be motivated by self-attention. (v.6)
The instruction to not come under bondage—or put another under bondage to us. (v. 9)
Allow God to work through you.

  Christ your example Eph. 5:1; John 10:27
  Not men pleasers   Col. 2:8
  Place full confidence in God's directives
    Phil. 2:12

  There is a difference in binding traditionalism and God's requirements.

Tradition + Change = Pressure + Guilt

Guilt imposed by others is usually caused by changes seen in you.

SCRIPTURE AND GUILT

Perhaps the most difficult of all guilt patterns are those self-imposed ones. The kind of thing that develops within you for having left the children overnight to go somewhere with your husband. The feeling of who and what priorities should come first. Should I leave the home responsibilities to pursue church and community involvements? If I do, I am under guilt for having neglected some other area of my life, at home, or in a spiritual sense.

The area of role conflicts can present itself as somewhat of a free-floating guilt. "I am neglecting one to do the other kind of feeling." So, it demands an honest approach to an ever-prevailing problem. Maybe, we should examine those role conflicts a little more closely. You can begin by trying to define them. What is your first and primary role? (Wife, employee, mother, church and community worker, or whatever.) List the major roles you are asked to fill.
EXAMPLE:

Wife	*Mother*	*Community*

Now, under each heading name the things you are expected to do, pertaining to that role.
EXAMPLE:

Wife	*Mother*	*Community*
listener	nurse	organizer
lover	chauffeur	taxi driver
etc.	etc.	cook, etc.

When you have done that, remind yourself that you are only one person (which might answer the question as to your fatigue). Decide which area in your report lists the activities which are most important to you. If you are married, the role of wife is always first, the others coming in order.

Next, take one of your major roles, and pull out (from the list of activities pertaining to that role) your *three highest priorities*. Decide the difference between activities which are "necessary" and those which are "vital" to your husband, employer, self, or spiritual life. When you have finished, your plan of action should look like this:

Wife

listener		
lover	1) lover	(List in
maid	2) listener	order of
partner	3) partner	priorities.)
confidante		

Establish the same type of priority listing for each major role you fill.

Role No. 1   Role No. 2   Role No. 3

Now that you have named those things that have to be done, put them under the proper role listing, start working on a schedule allocating time for the most essential. Investigate the possibility of assigning some of the responsibilities to another member of the family. Combine as many duties as you can, and begin working toward goals to relieve some of the pressures. Start learning your level of strengths and weaknesses! (. . . and we all have them.)

FURTHER PLAN OF ACTION

How to bring the three images into balance:

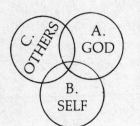

A. Peace with God brings peace with self.
   Heb. 13:20-21
   Rom. 5:1
   John 14:27

B. Strength for the inner self linked with God.
   Phil. 4:13
   2 Cor. 12:9-10
   The self finds a new Master.
   2 Cor. 5:15-17

C. A harmonious relationship develops between oneself, God and others.
   I Thess. 3:12
   I Pet. 1:22

1. Visualize yourself as a part of God's handiwork.
2. Settle yourself in a loving relationship with God, as your heavenly Father.
3. Begin now to start in a positive direction for building the inner self.
4. Distinguish the difference between imposed guilt, sin guilt, imaginary guilt.

Study the GUILT chart at the end of this chapter.

5. Get a better understanding of yourself by referring to the self-description test in chapter seven (page 94).

ALSO . . . . .
   A. Refuse to accept guilt
   B. Resolve guilt quickly
   C. Learn the areas of guilt

THREE AREAS OF GUILT ARE:

1. SIN GUILT as a result of one's need for salvation.

2. IMPOSED GUILT being transferred upon the person by another person or persons.

3. IMAGINARY GUILT taken upon oneself in relation to inner conflicts. Usually associated with roles, a break from tradition, or change in self-identity concept.

WHAT ABOUT SIN GUILT IN RELATION TO THE GOD IMAGE?

1. All have sinned and come short of the glory of God. Rom. 3:23

2. My part in resolving guilt is in confession with my mouth, believing with my heart, and verbalizing my faith, as based on the following scriptures: Romans 10:10-11; 1 John 1:9

3. God's part in dealing with the guilt is emphatic, and clearly stated.

   a) He will FORGIVE 1 John 1:9 Eph. 1:7
                                  Col. 1:14

   b) He will CLEANSE 1 Cor 6:11 Rev. 1:5
                Acts 11:9

   c) He is FAITHFUL to HIS PROMISE
             Heb. 10:23

4. Jesus' blood becomes the covering for our sins. They are completely blotted out . . . and we will never be judged by them.

THE BLOOD: THE INK BLOTTER FOR SIN

    Isa. 43:25   Eph. 1:7

5. There is no sin that can be visible through the blood of Jesus.

6. Sin guilt is transferred—cast away—never to be remembered against us again.

. . . THEN GOD SUFFERS AMNESIA . . . FORGETS

Heb. 10:16-17

GUILT

Three Kinds

SIN GUILT	IMAGINARY GUILT	IMPOSED GUILT
Romans 3:23-"For all have sinned, and come short of the glory of God" (KJV).	Feeling of God's wrath against you for human error.	Traditional & Cultural
		Christ's indictment to the Pharisees. Matt. 23:1-12
	God does not keep a tally sheet. Ps. 130:3-4	

SIN GUILT	IMAGINARY GUILT	IMPOSED GUILT
		1. Heavy externalism - v. 5
MY PART:		
1 John 1:9		2. Motivated by self-atten-tion - v. 6
Do What?		
Rom. 10:10		
	If we fail:	3. Not to come under bond-age or put another under
	1 John 2:1	bondage to us - v. 9

GOD'S PART:		
		Allow God to work through you by His Word.
1 John 1:9	Who is the Lawyer on your case?	
1. Forgive	1 John 2:1	1. Phil. 2:12
Eph. 1:7		
Col. 1:14		2. Not followers of men.
2. Cleanse	His mercies are new each	Col. 2:8
1 Cor. 6:11	morning!	
Rev. 1:5		3. Christ our example.
Acts 11:9	Lam. 3:22-23	Eph. 5:1-2
3. Faithful	"It is of the Lord's mercies	John 10:27
Mt. 24:35-"Heaven and	that we are not consumed,	
earth shall pass away, but	because his compassions fail	Have full confidence in God
my words shall not pass	not. They are new every	to direct you.
away" (KJV).	morning: great is thy faith-	
Isa. 55:7	fulness" (KJV).	THERE IS NO GUILT IN
		FORGIVENESS!

9

Who Is that Woman in the Mirror?

There is a sense in which you must learn to like yourself. This is not in an arrogant, haughty approach. It is simply learning to like what God created in you.

Let me ask, "Do you see yourself as being unique or as a Ho-Hum individual?"

What of this great *uniqueness*? No one in all the world was born with the innate potential you alone have! To lose this by submerging yourself into images of lost identity is to lose God's Divine purpose. To try and be someone outside of God's plan is to thwart the plan at work within you. Why? You are not yourself, what others expect, or what God wants.

In the truest sense, you become no one!

Did God make you? Sure he did!

"The Lord hath made ALL THINGS for Himself . . ." Prov. 16:4 KJV

"He fashioned us . . . " Ps. 119:73 KJV

He not only designed and fashioned you, he fitted the fabric of your life to the environmental circumstance that surrounds you, and it is He who designs the master plan.

Any woman knows the value of the garment is in its designer. The person who sews the label in the finished product represents his "original." What a terrible mistake we make trying to wear the label of another.

ILLUSTRATION:

My grandmother was a proud Dutch lady. She was also a very lovable, kind woman. We grandchildren loved climbing into her arms and cuddling into her oversize lap. It was like jumping into a feather bed! She was a beautiful seamstress, who tailored her own clothes, and carefully guarded the same as her well-dressed secret. However, it was always understood that when grandmother was having a special occasion, she wanted gifts purchased from the department store, never handmade!

My Aunt Bessie had a tremendous sense of humor. She would work for hours copying one of the originals of her day, making a gift for her mother. Then, she would rip the label from one of her own dresses and sew it into the garment being given Grandmother.

I still chuckle at the memory of the beautifully wrapped box and the zest with which it was opened. I can visualize her "strutting" in what she thought was the "haute couture" (most fashionable dress of the season). Grandma was fooled by her fun-loving daughter; but she respected the label and the workmanship of the dress.

What we see in the garment usually determines its care. The same is true as we see ourselves. God places eternal values on the person and calls each one of us "His originals." Not only that, He knows us as individuals.

So much so, that when you were created, the Lord took time out to count the hairs on your head (Matt. 10:30), ran the number through his "all-wise" computer and attached your name to the number.

I like the idea of God's individualized care for me as a person, not just a number, a real person! He never intended I lose that identity either . . . and . . . when I do I have spoiled His workmanship.

To everyone God gave abilities and talents. Wait a minute, you are about to say once more: "I don't have any!" Oh yes, you do! You may not have discovered them, but they are there. One thing is sure, you will never be measured by another's ability.

The parable of the talents (Matt. 25:4-30) gives us a good insight into what God considers our best. To one person He gives one talent; to another, two or three; another, five. But, the beautiful part is, each one is measured by his own talents. In the economy of God's measurements, two and two equal the equivalent of five and five. If it is our best! The reason: Jesus steps in and makes up the deficits.

God just doesn't pit one person against the other; and when we do it to ourselves, we feel limited, discouraged, and frustrated. As a growing person, we should see ourselves with needs that present to us an unlimited potential for growth. Again, Tim LaHaye emphasizes this by saying: "Everyone has an image of himself, either good or bad, but whatever that self-image, it affects our behaviour, attitudes, productivity, and ultimate success in life." [5]

5. Ibid., p. 137-138.

True, that self-image is often determined early in life. Everything that has touched you up to this point has been an "input," either negative or positive. The raw material of your training, background and environmental surroundings has helped to make up what psychologists call a frame-of-reference. That is what makes you the important person you are.

It is God who takes the years of past experience and threads them into your total personality. The many factors of the genes of your heredity add color and charm. Each thread of personal joy, suffering, happiness and pain add their part to the *great design of your life*. No one else has the *"wealth of your past"* to draw upon! You alone live within the set of present circumstances, and within the weaknesses and strengths of your own personality. And, you alone, can find a spiritual balance of acceptance between yourself and God. Remember! Everything God touches is touched for a Divine purpose and nothing is so good it cannot be made better by His touch!

I know, the pattern of your life may not be totally clear at any given moment. It is because God is still at work in you, perfecting the workmanship. It is up to Him to cut across the fabric of your life as He wills. The cutting of the selvage, the trimming of the seams, the lay of the fold and the pattern are all His responsibility. I believe . . .

> God can take the brush of His love, dip it into the chromatic colors of day-to-day experiences, from the palette of time, and produce a "masterpiece" within you!

Or, like a beautiful rosebud, He can open the petals

of your life upward toward Him, outward to others. So, begin today to draw strength from what He has given you. Use your intellect, and by faith be motivated toward some lasting goals. Although what you see in yourself now may be the result of your past, it is no excuse for the future. You alone determine where you will go from here! The sooner you start the better.

HOW?

1. Believe that everyone has something to give.
2. Learn the levels of your own interests and begin to personalize them into realities.
3. Look at your own God-given abilities.
4. Learn to accept temporary setbacks.
5. Pursue the "niche" of opportunity until it becomes a "door."
6. Have persistence of purpose.
7. Begin today to start tapping the well of your physical and spiritual resources.
8. Release the "total self" to be creative by accepting the past and integrating it into the present in a positive way.
9. Motivate yourself into action and "get with it" today.
10. Understand that just as the power of an atom is in its release, so is your potential.

A prayer for the "saint who feels life is a mystery":

> Well, forgive me Lord . . .
> I have struggled over the talent situation long enough. Maybe . . . it isn't so important that I am not able to do all the things others can do. I think you have finally gotten through to me!

Why, Lord, did those things seem so terribly important to me yesterday?

Today I see more clearly!

Now I know that I am still on your easel, and the picture of my life is not yet finished. Yesterday, my vision was limited. In the midst of my problem, all I could see were the bold splashes of color being stroked upon me by the finger of God. They appeared to me, at the time, to be mistaken colors of identity.

But . . . thanks, Lord, for the gentleness of your touch, for the soothing breath of the Holy Spirit. And . . . what a delightful discovery to know I am your masterpiece.

The bold brashness of my own inadequacy has been blended together upon the canvas of my heart. You have softened it with the intricate detailing of your delicate brush of time.

It may be that the picture will be completed soon . . . but . . . PLEASE LORD, KEEP ME ON THE EASEL UNTIL IT IS FINISHED!

PLAN OF ACTION

DO YOU SEE YOURSELF AS AN INDIVIDUAL?

Close your eyes and think!

What is the first word that comes to mind when you think of yourself? Write it._____ .
Is it positive?_____ Negative?_____Is the word a clue to your self-evaluation?

Read these verses and write down three positive things God says about you.

Ps. 139:13-16

1. _____
2. _____
3. _____

Is. 49:5

1. _____
2. _____
3. _____

Jer. 1:5

1. _____
2. _____
3. _____

Compare these: Ps. 139:14, 2 Tim. 2:20-21 with Jer. 31:3.

SELF-ACCEPTANCE WORKSHEET

List three things about yourself that you consider your greatest assets.

1._____
2._____
3._____

If you had the ability to change just ONE thing about yourself/life, what would it be?_____
_____

Why is it so important to you?_____
_____

If you were to make the change, would it help you in being:

1. More effective as a Christian?
2. A better wife?
3. A better mother/friend/companion?

How *IMPORTANT* are these changes to your effectiveness as a Christian? _____
_____

Take two minutes and write/list as many good qualities about yourself as you can think of:
_____

_____
_____
_____
_____

When someone last complimented you, how did you feel?

Silly_____Good _____ Cautious _____

Proud _____

Did you accept it genuinely graciously? _____
What were you complimented for? _____
Did you list this as one of your qualities? _____
READ:
Psalms 139:14-16, _____
I Thess. 1:4 _____
Rom. 9:20 _____

Unit III

Where Are You Going?

10

Where Do You Start?

There must be a beginning before there is progress. So let's talk about "how" and "where" to start.

How about beginning with honesty? And that ain't easy! In wanting to live up to all the things we are trying to be, we have built "air bubbles" around ourselves, afraid to expose the real person; afraid people won't like what they might see in us. So, we go right on building our barriers to keep people out. It is as if we are in some great "parade" of life.

The story is told of a poor little child who had lived to the age of twelve without seeing a parade. He worked hard all year to save enough money to pay his way to the city to watch the fanfare. Amidst the great excitement before the parade began, he stood with the crowd watching the clowns perform. When they had finished, he grabbed his little brother by the hand and headed for home; only to discover later, he had not observed the parade at all. He had only seen the confetti and carnival acts, without knowing the thrill of the main event.

The apostle Paul warned us about this possibility:

> Those in frequent contact with the ex-
> citing things the world offers should
> make good use of their opportunities
> without stopping to enjoy them"
> 1 Cor. 7:31 TLB

I am wondering if we, too, may be missing the real world by building our life-style on the confetti of the superficial. We become collectors of trivia, sour and defensive about everything. Knowingly or unknow-ingly, we hang a "DON'T TOUCH ME" sign on our psychological ego—closing ourselves in. So close, we find we cannot live within the circle of our own confinement; until finally, we are choked to death psychologically, spiritually and physically. There is no question about it, external behavior is a reflector of inner principle!

Like the old lady who sometimes baby-sat with my children. We called her Grandma R. On this one occasion, I had taken our older child, Deanna, to Grandma's house for the evening. After having instructed Deanna to give proper respect, and not to ask a lot of questions of the elderly woman, I left her driveway with both fingers crossed—hoping my orders would be obeyed! Sure enough, I found out later that I had hardly closed the door when the series of questioning began. My little urchin walked right up to Grandma, put both of her hands upon her tiny hips and said: "I know I am not supposed to ask any questions, 'cause my mommy told me not to. There is just one thing I would like to know—"

Grandma R. looked right into the face of the four-year-old and said, "Just shoot!" (That was her special way of telling you to say anything that came into your mind.)

Upon that invitation to speak, Dee took one full turn, fastened her eyes on the living room walls, and asked: "I would just like to know where you got all of this junk?"

You must understand that the woman was a collector of mottos (which did not justify the remark made by my daughter, and we took care of her—at a much later time—when I overheard Grandma R. chuckling as she related the incident to our church women's group). I think the old lady had kept every calendar from year one, each on top of the other, since her wedding day.

It was most evident she was living in the past. Every memento on her wall was a reminder to her of bygone years.

(You know, I learned that even good memories are not to be the *"house in which one lives"* but the *"avenue through which one passes."* Sure, we should revisit them occasionally, and draw strength from those remembrances of past joys! The problem is: When we keep trying to move back into yesteryear, we find few new "joys" in the todays.)

The cluttered walls of that home are not unlike many persons with whom I have talked. They can remember their hurts and hang them like "prize trophies" on the mental walls of their minds. Any conversation you start with them eventually turns to the "soured leftover" memories of the past. To speak of your personal joy is like rubbing salt in their wounds, for they are constant reminders, to you, of how hard life has been for them.

There comes a time when we must consider our past as analogous to leaves off a tree. We have the choice of either using them (past experiences) like a mulch to fertilize the brightest rosebud, or consider them as a wasted nuisance. If it is true, and I believe it is, that into every life a little rain must fall; then, you are the deciding factor as to how you will be affected. Do you become bitter and resentful, or do you determine to live each day as an exciting venture into new and lasting relationships? Sure you are going to get hurt. That is the only way you learn to live! But, when you close yourself off, hiding behind masks of superficial trivia, you never know the thrill of sharing, giving a part of yourself.

It is so easy to get bogged down in self-pity that it becomes impossible to enjoy another person's dreams, or feel their pain and to laugh with them. I haved summed it up this way:

Self-Pity

I pity . . . I pity
    Those who pity not me.
Me, is to be pitied you see.
    You want me . . . to pity thee?
How can I . . .
    When I am pitying me?

A friend of mine encourages women to cancel what he calls, "pity parties." I kinda like his definition!

SHED THE MASKS

There are so many masks we learn to hide behind. Like the one of intellectualism, the all-head-and-no-heart feeling of analytical reasoning that seems to have all the answers to life. The aire of mental superiority some persons project, immediately isolates them from the so-called average. I am not sure about that philosophy!

It is somewhat like the incident of the young theology student who went into the country to minister at a small church during the absence of its pastor. He is said to have taken the pulpit in his flowing clerical robe. After having poised himself with a long look heavenward, he proceeded to pray—

"Oh thou, Omnipotent One. Holy Potentate, only begotten one of the divine universe. To Thee, the Omniscient Benefactor of all mankind, and . . . thou, O Lord, what else shall I call thee?"

His prayer was suddenly interrupted by an old lady sitting on the front row.

"Try callin' 'em your heavenly Father and askin' Him to do sumpin' fer you," she said.

What a lesson in intellectual pretension, and what a thrill it is to find someone who is nothing more-or-less than one's own refreshing self.

We are still having to watch out for those extremes. Either we are all-head-and-no-heart, or all-heart-and-no-head! Wouldn't it be great if we could live within a balance, even in these areas of intellectualism and emotion?

BALANCE?

God dealt with balance in the creation of the

universe. Take a look at this old planet earth. How long do you think it would keep on spinning if it went all "awry," got out of balance and rotated right off its axis? Not very long I am sure! You need only to examine the trees with their symmetry, the rosebud and its petals, and the tiny nodes of the flower stem, to understand God's perfect unity in nature. Solomon, the wise man, recognizes this principle when he wrote these words:

> "To everything there is a season, and a time to every purpose under the heaven:
>
> A time to be born, and a time to die; a time to plant, and a time to pluck up that which is planted;
>
> A time to weep, and a time to laugh; a time to mourn, and a time to dance.
> Eccles. 3:1,2,4 KJV

I think this shows a great insight into the very nature of God Himself. Most of us have to learn how to laugh with those who laugh, and discover the wonderful quality of being able to sorrow with those who know sorrow.

Thermostat or Thermometer—Which?

Once you have learned to bring yourself into *balance* and shed the masks that cover the real you, there will be a release for growing maturity. It brings with it a sense of self-value, making you a kind of thermostat to your environmental surroundings.

There seem to be two kinds of women: those who do little more than register the feelings about them (they just react to external circumstances); and others—who do much more than that—they change the temperature of the situation! The self-fulfilled woman is able to live through chaos because she knows it is only a passing thing. The one who is bound up in her own feelings is unable to see beyond the "today" and is only a thermometer of the present. So, she accepts chaos, internalizing it into her psyche.

REACTIVE COVERINGS

Burying those feelings of turmoil adds only another dimension of barriers. We find ourselves all bound up! The only form of release from the situation is to react in several different ways. I will mention three of them here:

The "vesuvian" personality does nothing more in life except pour skyward fiery lava, at the least suspecting intervals. She burns the beauty right out of her life and others.

If you have ever been on the islands of Hawaii you can understand what this is like. I stood at the base of a volcano there, looking at the remains of molten rock and a few scroungy shrubs that had survived the ordeal. I wondered at the internal pressure that could produce such an outburst.

Not only that, as we visited the mouth of the large crater, we were told of the apprehensions of those living nearby, because of their not knowing when the next "big spill" would come.

What a tragedy!

Another kind of response is the "garbage bag" personality who gathers up all the data of past hurts, disappointments and sorrows, and dumps them out on the least-suspecting persons. Usually, the victim is the one who is closest to the reactor at the time. The hurt is projected over and onto the non-suspecting victim as transferred hostility. The receiving victim may be totally innocent. All of us have done this at some time in our lives. We have lashed out against another when they, in fact, had absolutely nothing to do with the situation in which we were involved. (Even if they had, that does not justify rationalizing away our actions).

Another response that is most evident is the "barbed wire" attack—the sharp tongue of criticism, the catty remarks that accentuate the cutting personality. After being in the presence of some women, I have gone home feeling the need of a mental de-fusing; I wanted to brush my teeth or bathe myself. On the other hand, I have walked from the presence of others, who made me feel better. They lifted my spirits, gave me a sense of beauty, an attitude of inner serenity. What makes the difference? Is it because one has never known pain or disappointment? No, I am afraid not! I discovered there are a few characteristics the latter hold in common with all "growing persons." They had:

1. Learned to be peacemakers by refusing to add their opinions to a situation they could do nothing about.
2. Refused to build a life-style on the hurts, using them as stepping-stones for growth.
3. Learned the beautiful art of knowing how to laugh with people and not at them.
4. Could compliment others openly and freely without feeling it to be a threat against themselves.

5. Could settle their differences, disagree without being disagreeable.
6. Learned something from everyone they met, regardless of who it was.
7. Tried to live naturally, unpretensiously, within the framework of their own personality.
8. Made a place for themselves by their mental attitude of positive faith.
9. Could make friends by first showing themselves friendly.
10. HAD LEARNED TO LAUGH AT THEM-SELVES . . . knowing that humor solves many of the problems of life.

PLAN OF ACTION FOR THE MOST SUPERIOR/ INFERIOR PERSONALITY

Fleshly inferiority is ruled by feelings of the base impulses. Superiority is a covering of those base impulses!

Fleshly Inferiority vs. True Humility

Self-righteous masks of transferred responsibility	Isa. 64:6 KJV Our righteousness is as filthy rags.
2 Cor. 10:12 Comparison with others is a fleshly habit that makes for false security in thinking oneself as good as average, or less than average.	Jer. 17:9 KJV The heart is deceitful above all things, and desperately wicked: who can know it?

Inferiority of oneself should be labeled as God labels it . . . PRIDE!

I - insecurity
N - negativism
F - failure
E - envious
R - resentment
I - internal ear
O - overly sensitive
R - reactor to people
I - insecurity
T - tension
Y - yielding to self-pity

John 8:32

The truth sets us free . . . as we learn the truth of God's Word, we are able to recognize our true position in Him.

God made no person inferior to another.

"Man makes man inferior"

Ps. 139:14

1. Inferiority is merely an attitude! Attitudes can be changed if you want them changed.
2. No one can make you feel inferior without your consent . . . Eleanor Roosevelt.
3. Direct your feelings of inadequacies toward God, who made you. You cannot love Him . . . and hate what He created!

11

Going Where With Whom?

ILLUSTRATION:

One of my most embarrassing moments occurred at the burial of a dear lady, who had been a long-standing member of our church.

My husband was called back, after having been transferred to another area, to conduct the funeral services for the woman's family.

There was a deacon's wife, of whom I was particularly fond, and so we decided to ride together from the church to the burial site. Like typical women, the two of us quickly engaged ourselves in an animated conversation. Our car was about midway in the procession.

We drove along, getting caught up on the happenings of the past few years, when suddenly the procession in front of us took a sharp left turn. Unconsciously, I went straight ahead! Of course, all of the cars behind were following me. You guessed it! I was leading the last half of the funeral cortege in the wrong direction.

Luckily for us, the friend riding with me knew the route to the cemetery. We pulled up to the intersection going west and met the hearse with the other automobiles arriving from the south.

I could have said, "Hey look, I am leading this parade," but I had to face up to the problem of going in the wrong direction. Even so, life has a lot of "detour-ish" mishaps. Yet, everyone is going somewhere.

And, we have all been, at some time or other, "side-tracked" on the "road-of-life." We have momentarily lost our sense of direction. Oftentimes, it is there on the side roads of a new experience that real and lasting lessons are learned. In most cases, it is then that we really begin to learn how to live, to appreciate help from others, and to develop friendships that blossom into meaningful human relationships.

"FRIENDSHIP'S GARDEN"

While walking through my Garden of Friends
   I stopped to rest for a bit.
To admire each floral beauty
   and the life it so aptly spent.
Turning my head in amazement
   Standing before my eyes.
Was a daffodil gracefully lifting
   Its tiny face to the skies.
The poised serenity of its petals
   Calmed my heart that day.
The flower had been planted, by a friend
   Who knew I would be coming that way.

A violet was blooming in perfect silence

'Neath a tall and stately rose,
With no thought of being unnoticed,
   Serving in quiet repose.
The face of a sturdy sunflower
   Stopped, bending its leafy head.
A carnation whispered to it kindly
   About what the petunia had said.

Each flower was yielding its fragrance
   Giving its beauty free.
I stood . . . absorbing the perfumes
   My friends were imparting to me.

Ruthe White

If you think you can make it through life totally independent of others, then you had best examine the direction in which you are headed. Why? Again, Solomon speaks to us about our interdependence upon others, our need for people.

> Two are better than one, because they have a good [more satisfying] reward for their labor;
>
> For if they fall, the one will lift up his fellow. But woe to him who is alone when he falls and has not another to lift him up. Eccle. 4:9, 10 Amplified

How very important it is—learning to live with other people, to make new friends, to appreciate the not-so-new friendships and to accept all persons as a vital part of one's growing self. The happiest people I have observed in life are those who have learned to love and to open themselves up toward others.

I think of FRIENDSHIPS AS A BEAUTIFUL GARDEN . . . with each flower blooming independently within its own species, each plant feeding from the nutrients of its God-given soil.

The beauty of friendship can be visualized in a beautiful arrangement of flowers. The skillful hands of the florist will carefully choose three yellow roses, placing them just right to give the needed height. She will scatter a few sprigs of heather with a handful of daisies, using a touch of baby's breath to frame it in. She places each flower to give it the greatest advantage for showing its natural beauty. One color accentuates the other giving balance, beauty, and symmetry to the bouquet.

Friends are given for a landscape to our lives—like flowers lifting their lofty petals toward the sunlight of God's grace, blending their aromas, absorbing the fragrance of others, giving and receiving, knowing that they, too, are a part of God's great handiwork.

I think this was the great secret of Christ's successful ministry. He knew how to receive as well as give; to accept the loving relationships of those about Him. What do you think attracted people to Jesus? Was it simply because He was the Messiah? No! Our Lord was also human. It was this human element that made Him desire the friendship of the family in Bethany. No wonder He wept at the tomb of Lazarus. He felt the loss of His friend as keenly as any of us would have.

There was something about our Lord that attracted others toward Him. Sure, He was the Messiah, but His Messiahship was not revealed until the latter part of His life and ministry. Prior to Jesus' baptism in the River Jordan by John the Baptist, He had moved in the regular flow of the culture of His day. Christ was not a freak, recluse, or withdrawn from the mainstream of society. The Scripture indicates that His life was so modestly normal, it was impossible for many to accept Him as the Messiah.

When the Lord appeared at Jordan, to be baptized by John, there was a mutual appreciation of relationship. There seems to have been no dialogue between them verbally at the time. However, John summed it all up later by giving us this beautiful insight into Christ's character: "He shall not strive . . ." Matt. 12:19 KJV

There was never a competitive attitude on the part of either of them toward each other. Neither of them had anything to prove! John had come to prepare the way for Christ; Christ was becoming the fulfillment of John's ministry.

The Lord had the tremendous ability to make friends. He accepted their human weaknesses and strengths without feeling threatened by them. He knew full well that one of the disciples would betray Him. He took that calculated risk! Judas was given the full rights and privileges of all the other followers of Christ, although he was to be the betrayer. There were times when it appears Jesus went a little beyond the call of reason in relation to Judas. It seems ridiculous to think He would place the clan's savings account in the "Bank of Judas." Why did Jesus need him? It was because Judas needed Christ much more than the Lord needed him. Matthew was good at computing interest rates. His expertise with the "Internal Revenue" speaks for itself. Why could the tax collector not have been chosen as the treasurer?

I am glad He chose poor Judas! Of course, the

Scripture had to be fulfilled, but what a beautiful example in building interpersonal relationships. Involvement with people requires a certain amount of blind faith. There is always that risk of being sabotaged, hurt, misunderstood and, yes, betrayed. For this reason, many people set out to reach their goals in life totally independent of others. When this happens, a terrible spirit of fear, reprisal and broken confidences binds our spirit personalities. We would rather do nothing toward building friendships than take those chances of being hurt. The results are extremely hazardous!

Everybody needs somebody and that somebody is you.

We all have a tendency to want to insulate ourselves from hurts. In so doing, we close off our greatest opportunity for growth and personality development. One common method used is that of *withdrawal*: By staying away from people, refusing to build any personal commitments, we build a false sense of security. So, by failing to take on responsibilities involving others, we build *barriers* to keep people out. Eventually, those very fences will prove to be our greatest enemies. They will squeeze us like a murderous strangler, or be like a thief who steals our prize possessions.

One of the greatest "blessings" in the work of God in our hearts, is to recognize that He can help us in this area of our lives. There is no burden heavier than the millstone of self-consciousness; nothing so easy to fasten onto as our misery; nothing so apt to produce self-pity than suffering; nothing that will separate us from others as quickly as the sin of self-involvement. When we begin to close ourselves off from others, it becomes a settled habit. We become saturated with our own misery. The very act of letting go of ourselves lifts us into a higher plane of living. It releases us to feel when other people hurt, letting others sense when we are hurting.

Closed-Circle Friendships

What are some of the barriers that hinder friendships? Let me begin by saying: Women who are afraid to build strong bonds of friendship with others may have a tendency to gravitate toward *one-friend-only*. One-to-one sharing can be a very meaningful experience, or it can be stifling. Caution

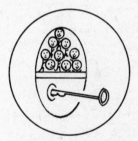

CLOSED-CIRCLE
One group is locked in to keep another out.

must be taken that a person does not become possessive of the one close friend, that is, to the exclusion of others. There is a tendency to become jealous, and resentful, if the one friend begins to break away or to accept another person into their one-to-one relationship.

Another kind of woman is the one who is so insecure in herself that she may—to seek to prove her acceptability or win approval—become the social leader. She is all things to all people, never knowing the thrill of a one-to-one relationship. Her repertoire of roles will run the gamut of every involvement in the community or church activities.

Church ladies are often caught in this vicious circle *of doing and out doing!* Their friendships are often based on self-likes: doing the things we like to do, sharing with those who fit into our molds, excluding new persons, and working on things that involve those within our own little circle.

Clique Friendships

Clique friendships are very much the same. Except in the clique church club situation, one strong personality usually emerges as the leader. She calls the signals, forming a satellite group around her. The minute her leadership is threatened, she will seek to influence the group.

CLIQUE TYPES

Based on self-likes.

SATELLITE

Dominated by one strong personality manipulating the weaker.

Persons with weaker personalities tend to gravitate toward this type of relationship. It becomes easy for them to find acceptance within the peer group, so long as they remain a follower. The minute the leader's position is endangered, she will begin to manipulate the weaker personality thus controlling those within her clique. If a new person emerges, moving toward the group, she represents a threat to the leadership and so is scrutinized and often squeezed out.

Churches and small community groups, as well as clubs with strong standing memberships, are most susceptible to this kind of strong inner clique groups. This also affects the growth of the unit and the individuals involved. A woman who feels she is rejected by one group will tend to move toward another. If she is a strong personality, she may even build her own counter group for the sake of survival. Small exclusive units begin to take place within the larger body: this leaves the new women in the church or community isolated from the mainstream of activity. Each group stands waiting to see which one will take the new person in. They often fight over who will win the friendship. The minute one circle accepts her, she is then dropped by the others.

Freedom of friendship should be our goal! We must allow others to move freely back and forth. We must be able to draw from one spiritual friendship to another. We need to feed and to be fed by the nectar of each beautiful life around us, and to learn from those whose lives we touch. As we grow together there must be great caution that we do not build this upon a facade.

Facade Friendships

Facade friendships fall into three philosophies of life. The parable of the good Samaritan (Luke

10:30-37) depicts these attitudes toward neighborly relationships.

"I see you but I have no time for you," is a common attitude in today's culture. Self-involvement with our own families takes precedence over the needs of others, making us oblivious to the people around us.

"Because you have nothing I need, I have not the time for you" is another approach of human rationale. We are so guilty of judging the other person's ability by what we first see, never recognizing the real person, never knowing the possibility of their strengths for positive reinforcement into our lives. "Because you have something I need, I will take it" is the practice used most commonly in day-to-day relationships. We become like a parasite.

Parasitical Friendships

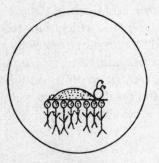

PARASITICAL

Getting, never giving— then casting them away.

One of my pet peeves is to see a woman who is *parasitical* in her friendships, taking all another has to give, giving nothing in return. She leeches onto the very lifestream of her friends, placing unreasonable demands upon them, using them to her own advantage. After her cause is best served, she moves on to another unfortunate victim, repeating the same pattern over and over.

Two persons are responsible for this kind of situation: the parasite, and the one who allows it to happen to them. Unfortunately, there are those who seem to enjoy being used, and those who delight in using them. "Approvalitis" is the word! The victim is seeking acceptance and approval. Because of this, they will go beyond the call of duty to prove themselves worthy of the other person's friendship. The person becomes a slave to everyone, and is willing to be a martyr for fear of rejection by her peers. When the person attempts to cut away from the group and refuses to accept another assignment, a major psychological warfare may ensue. One person's assertion of finding acceptance outside the group may become the other person's threat.

Friendships should not be measured on the scales of human materialism. James warned us against this. He said:

> If a man comes into your church dressed in expensive clothes and with valuable gold rings on his fingers, and at the same moment another man comes in who is poor and dressed in threadbare clothes, and you make a lot of fuss over the rich man and give him the best seat in the house and say to the poor man, "You can stand over there if you like, or else sit on the floor"—well, judging a man by his wealth shows that you are guided by wrong motives. James 2:2-4 TLB

Many of us must guard ourselves against this

temptation of misplaced values. There are times in which we need to stop and reevaluate the principles that govern our actions. There are cycles in a woman's life when she might be even more vulnerable to this temptation of materialism. I deal with that in a later chapter, under the "cycle changes" of life.

Years ago, a little lady sauntered into our church. She was weak and emaciated looking, frail with a shy personality. My first impression, after trying to counsel with her, was to write her off. I felt she was totally incapable of receiving my friendship or contributing anything positive toward mine. A few months elapsed in time before our paths crossed again. At which time, through the least-suspecting manner, I discovered that we shared many of the same interests. Since then a bond of friendship has developed between us, unlike that of any other of my friends. When I think of what I could have missed so easily, I feel embarrassed and ashamed before God. Most of the greatest blessings in my life have come from the least-suspecting persons.

It is my feeling that we need friends of all ages, both young and old, from all walks of life. People of varied backgrounds add color and balance to one's personality, broadening one's intellect. They may also provide a strong supportive role in times of emotional or spiritual need.

Maintaining friendships should be important to everyone! I have observed older people who have many friends. They are healthier, happier, and much more adjusted to life than those who have chosen to isolate themselves. It has been suggested that a retired person should write at least one letter each day. There is something about that personal touch with people that creates a psychological lifeline. It is important that we take a little time out of our lives to give, to give until it hurts, without expecting anything in return. Life then becomes an "echo" bringing back that which was given.

12

Do You Know Your Own Resources?

All life is mirrored in the mind.
--Cicero

The mind, or intellect, is God's gift to you. Thus, the power of the "reasoning will," submitted to God, becomes a reservoir of His untapped potential in you. That fact alone should motivate you to discipline your mind into a positive direction for mental and spiritual growth; also knowing, the failure to do so becomes a waste of human resource.

Just how much that waste is no one knows, because there is no adequate measuring device of the mental faculties. The very best known scientific methods for probing the brain are still faulty and incomplete. And, they cannot measure the human will!

Einstein says that, on the average, we use only ten percent or less of our actual brain power. If that is a fact, then, think how much would be done if we could develop the other ninety percent in a positive manner!

David Sarnoff, while a young man, recognized his own potential mental powers when he said: "Anything the mind can conceive it can do." He seemed to live by the principle he taught, and as messenger boy working for the Commercial Cable Company, David learned the Morse Code. The efforts of his work paid off! He was the first operator to pick up the distress signal of the sinking *Titanic* ship; also the first businessman to see the future in the radio and television industry.

It would appear to me, that the "LAW OF LIFE" is: "Whatever you wish to do—or be—must first be settled in the mind." Because of this, there is an unfleshly warfare over this great human potential. We ourselves decide how our mind will be used, either disciplined or if it will "run wild." If the garden of the mind is left uncultivated it will produce seeds that choke out the beauty of the inner soul. The Bible states: "We become what we think." (See Prov. 23:7.) And, I believe, everything about us reflects the pattern of our thought life.

ILLUSTRATION:

Abraham Lincoln, in seeing the portrait of another man, exclaimed, "I don't like him!" The puzzled gentleman to whom he spoke replied "Mr. Lincoln, I have never known you to be a man of prejudgment. Upon what basis do you make that statement?"

"Oh, but you see," Abe said, "his countenance reflects what he has been thinking, and it is bad."

You may be about to say: "That is totally unfair!" Is it really? It is sometimes difficult to understand that every visual image, verbal message, and all mental learning is deposited in the subconscious. Regardless of how this data is obtained, it is nevertheless stamped upon the mind. One field of psychology calls the mind an empty tablet, or slate, at the time of birth, with each thought pattern imprinting itself there indelibly. Assuming that to be true, it becomes terribly important what goes into the brain. Obviously, we must feed good things into the "memory bank" to receive back positive pictures for mental reinforcement to our inner principles.

If you refer back to the sociological chart, mentioned earlier, (page 106) you can understand better what I am saying: Today's cultural *norms* are not always geared toward developing positive aspects for good mental behavior. Since that is true, why then, are we so shocked when these negative images we have seen are mirrored back to us?

Power of the Visual Mind

Another example of this can be observed by what is internalized through the visual eye gate. The maturing woman, who seeks to maintain a spiritual level, will be on guard lest she break down the moral fibers of her own well-being by a form of attrition; a wearing away, and the tendency to conform, either consciously or subconsciously, with society's norms.

Look at what can happen in the average 30-minute soap opera. Three babies are being born out of wedlock, conceived by a man other than the women's husbands . . . or by mutual agreement of living together outside of the marriage contract. One of the prospective mothers is contemplating an abortion. The father of her baby is a well-known doctor who is carrying on an affair with an older woman. The lady with whom he is involved is being treated by a psychiatrist (who has fallen in love with her), after she has tried to commit suicide from having murdered her first husband. This twisted relationship goes on-and-on through a list of characters, involving conniving schemes to end family relationships, and giving a distorted image of what real love is all about. The married woman will find herself comparing her spouse to the man of the "celluloid" tape. This is most unfair! By the time her husband enters the door she is already conditioned to expect certain responses from him that may be totally unrealistic. He, then, is expected to kiss, caress, and fondle the woman who has spent her mental energies in self-absorbed thought; and, in many cases, she is emotionally drained and sometimes oblivious to his needs.

Sure, we are human—with physical and psychological needs—but feeding one's mind on the illicit affairs of others, on a day-to-day basis, will not meet them; nor, will it build strong marital ties and spiritual guidelines of restraint.

Sometimes we so-called spiritual ones like to hide behind our facades of pseudo-spirituality, thinking ourselves aloof from such earthly things as physical temptation. Not so! We may be even more vulnerable than our nonreligious sister, because we are unaware of our own vulnerability and we consider ourselves above falling. We go right on in the trappings of "sainthood," never taking an objective look at the real person hidden there.

We are often shocked to discover what the subconscious has filed away! When it surfaces, in the form of temptation, it becomes even more frightening. It is then, we must face up to ourselves and understand this is a weak area that is being exposed to the conscious mind. Otherwise, there would be no temptation.

Coping with Temptation

1. *Confess* it as being a need, and label it either legitimate or illegitimate.
2. *Replace* it with another form of self-fulfillment. Use Christ as your example by replacing the negative thought patterns with the positive . . . "Thus saith the Word!" Put your *will* into action. You, yourself, gird up the mind.
3. *Examine* it. Look at the temptation objectively as being a slice of the real self. See it as another step toward spiritual maturity.
4. *Look away* from it. Start looking upon Jesus.
5. Use the conscious conviction of the Spirit as a *mental eyelash* like a fringe of the inner soul, protecting it from spiritual irritants.

Human with Human Emotions

One of the first steps for the *maturing woman*, is to recognize she is human, with human emotions and physical desires like all other women. It is around those areas of need that most of her spiritual problems will develop (as mentioned in chapter five). Temptation arises when needs are not met by the husband, family, friends and society. The woman who is not taught, or does not know how to go to God for her inner strength, may blunder through life never knowing the difference between the transitory feeling of being *tempted*, and the act of yielding.

Every woman has thoughts, occasionally, that are not in harmony with her own inner convictions. She may even feel God's wrath. Therefore, for her to admit those needs may seem to her as an admission of weakness. Even guilt! Remember, a confession of need in any area of one's life is always good. It is not the admission of wrongdoing. The important thing is not whether you have a need, but the manner in which you fulfill that need.

The Christian woman will seek to keep her individual needs in balance within the framework of biblical teachings, and her own culture. How?

THE SPIRITUALLY-ORIENTED PERSONALITY . . .

1. Will develop a balanced life-style that keeps her steady as a self-fulfilled woman.

2. Her life patterns will be those oriented in Christ's teachings.

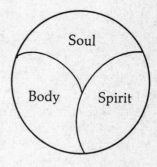

3. Actions will be motivated by Christian principles and her life will be absorbed in them.

4. Her body, soul, and spirit - self will find growth to its fullest potential. Although that growth is gradual, it will be an ongoing thing, not limited by age or circumstance.

THE SELF-CONTROLLED PERSONALITY . . .

1. Is motivated by the base nature, finding it easy to conform to cultural morals and standards.

2. Physical needs of self-controlled life take precedence over the spiritual.

3. Needs are internalized toward selfish interests as spiritual life diminishes.

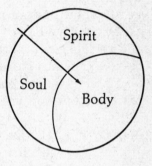

How are these implemented? You must recognize the work of God within you as He deals with your conscience (super-ego). I think of it in this manner:

Pattern of Development

God prompts the subconcious, prodding it into action.
By the choice of our will we decide what we will do about it.
If we decide to react toward a change of habits, effort is required.
Repetition of the act makes it easier.
Each time it is repeated, it requires less effort.
A habit is formed.
A life-style is developed.

Patterns for Growth

Among all living things, we alone have the ability to decide what our lives will be, and what we will do with our lives. We can change our minds about what we wish to make of them. Each person has the God-given ability to consciously shape the time that lies between his first breath of life and the last heartbeat before death.

Society would have us believe we have it made, and are home safe if we get married in our early 20s, have our children raised and educated by the time we reach our 40s, and are "settled in" before having reached the menopause years. Don't you believe it!

The *growing woman* never feels she has arrived. Norma Zimmer, the well-known singer of the "Lawrence Welk Show," talks about her ongoing need for voice lessons. She says she still practices every day and repeatedly goes back for more training. Perhaps that is the secret of her beauty and poise. She knows what she wants to accomplish and is not afraid to go out there, admit her need, and work toward her goals.

The headlines of the local newspaper carried a story recently about one of our local residents. She was a black woman who, after having reached the age of 80 years, decided to do something she had always wanted to do—go back to school and get her college degree. She did it and was being honored by her classmates for her contribution in education.

A popular trade magazine has just featured a challenge, to all persons of all ages, by showing a ratio of figures of the number of millionaires who had made their millions after passing the middle age years. The figure was pleasantly astonishing!

This leads me to believe that self-fulfillment is up to the individual. Each person passes through a time in life when the urge "hits." It strikes some younger than others. The time is not nearly so important as the goal toward which one is headed. For, at varying points, each one of us begins to sense the need for extending one's inner self.

Women keep saying to me: "It's too late. By the time I accomplished what I would like to, I would be too old to enjoy it." Nonsense! Will it make you any younger if you don't? You will be no older having started than you will be if you don't. You might be even younger, especially at heart! I am afraid too many of us go through life as if it were an endurance contest. Thoreau, the philospher, once talked about this very thing. He said, "The mass of men lead lives of quiet desperation."

Of all people, of any known time, who has the opportunity for reaching their goals it is the twentieth century Christian woman. Wherever the gospel of Jesus Christ has been preached, the role of the woman has always been elevated. It is no less true in this our day. Look at the number of times Jesus healed women, conversed with them, ate at their table, identified with his mother, and talked about those who had ministered to him in his earthly life. Remember! It was a woman who was the last to leave the scene of the Crucifixion, and the first to go to the closed sepulchre to anoint his body after the burial. She was also the first to see Jesus after his resurrection.

This thought alone should elevate your thinking to a place of personal self-worth. It should also give you a vision, goals for dimensional growth. There are three questions you might ask yourself in relation to the development of your mental and spiritual resources; and I think self-fulfillment comes in the recognition of these.

WHAT IS MY VISION?

Every woman needs three: A vision of where she has been; one of where she is now; and the other one, a vision of where she wants to go. If there is no target you will shoot at nothing and hit it every time.

Like the lady at one of our church business meetings who stood to give her report to the committee. "Well!" she said, "I have done absolutely nothing these past three months, and I have done it all right here in this church."

I think everyone should have some ongoing project toward which life is directed. The apostle Paul talked about a prize, a mark. I know he was speaking about his call and spiritual things when he said: ". . . This one thing I do . . ." Phil. 3:13 KJV

Somehow I think the same principle applies to all life. Everyone should have, or do, something that is uniquely theirs to enjoy and have, or do. There is an elixir and thrill in looking at that something and being able to say: "Wow! That looks great and I did it!"

What that something is, is not nearly so important as doing it and doing it well. If it is in typing a letter, and that is a source of pleasure to you, do it well. Whether it is designing a dress, or scrubbing the kitchen floor, finish the task so you can take pleasure in it. When the mop is hung back on its hook, kick off your shoes and enjoy the "squeak" as your toes touch the polished efforts.

We are told that Arnold Palmer, the great golfer, envisioned himself as such by the time he was 10 years of age. He thought of himself as a winner and imagined that announcers were calling off his name at the end of the game. John F. Kennedy, the late president, studied the life of Franklin Roosevelt and patterned his strategy with the goals of the presidency in mind. We all know he reached those goals at a very young age.

HOW WILL I MAKE THE VISIONARY GOALS A REALITY?

Can you believe that God would like to use you in a very special way? Whatever the method or in the least-suspecting way, always look for and expect a miracle. Quit fighting life and begin to cooperate with God, by living in every room of your physical, spiritual self. Decide now, today, how you are going to think! Either we plan monuments for the protection of our self-ego, or we choose to build on a mental foundation of inner principle that is ongoing, upon which a memorial of "righteousness" rests. The mind that is stretched toward reaching intrinsic goals is usually too busy to think about building some great monument of self-aggrandizement. Creativity itself becomes the rewarding element that makes a place for itself as one's goals are visualized. So, decide now what short-range goals you wish to achieve, correlate those with your immediate ones, and direct both of them toward an extended goal.

CAN I MAKE TIME WORK FOR ME?

Time is either our salvation or the proverbial "waterloo." Either we choose, arbitrarily, to go through life all bound up in tension; or, we recognize time is so precious, deal with our stresses and learn to hang loose. The Chinese talk about taking the emergencies of life leisurely.

The importance of each day should never be

minimized! So, plan it wisely! Develop the habit of mentally organizing your day before getting out of bed in the morning. While you are having a second cup (of whatever) jot down on a piece of paper those things you must do. (If you are like me, you will probably end up using the corner of your paper table napkin for the list.) Anyway, write them down and allow for some interruptions.

Don't let your schedule run you, you run the schedule. Take advantage of the days in which the adrenalin is flowing, rest out the bad ones, and plan on the upswing of a better day. While you are resting from the normal routine of "drudgery" go through some decorator books, try a new hairstyle, check your wardrobe and study your physical limitations. No one is made of iron. Remember it was from dust God made man! Understand that limitations in physical strength are relevant, so pace yourself according to what you can do.

THE "GOAL" MINE

1. Make goals that are "elastic," that stretch you but don't break you.
2. Have goals that are honest with "pins" for implementation.
3. Measure your ability with an honest "yardstick."
4. Use a big "thimble" as an insulation against the pricks of life.
5. Sew your dreams together with a "nylon thread," blending each life experience with an invisible bond for reaching goals.
6. Add a "pearl button," the Pearl of Great Price, for through Him all things can be done.

DRAW A ROUGH DRAFT OF YOUR DAY'S SCHEDULE

Mark 1:35	And in the morning, rising up a great while before day, he went out, and departed into a solitary place, and there prayed.
Luke 6:12	. . . in those days . . . he went out into a mountain to pray, and continued all night in prayer to God.

MORNING: 8:00 - 9:00 9:00 - 10:00	(Which time of your day) is busiest?
10:00 - 11:00 11:00 - 12:00	Which time of day is least interrupted?
AFTERNOON: 12:00 - 1:00 1:00 - 2:00 2:00 - 3:00	At which time are you most alert?: A.M. _____ P.M. _____
3:00 - 4:00 4:00 - 5:00 5:00 - 6:00	When do you have your quiet time? Approximate A.M. _____ hour you usually have P.M. _____ devotions:
EVENING: 6:00 - 7:00 7:00 - 8:00 8:00 - 9:00	(Do you have a definite) Time? _____ Place? _____

List free time activities:	Do they make you feel:		Do these activities refresh you:		
	Happy?	Depressed?	Physically?	Mentally?	Spiritually?
1)					
2)					
3)					
4)					
5)					

Which do you feel you take care of most:

The spiritual appetites?_____   Carnal desires?____

How many faith-building books and articles have you read this past month? _____

My spiritual pledge to God:

To guard closely the reins of my heart by giving God a chance to minister to my own spiritual needs as I endeavor to move into new dimensions in Him through prayer, Bible reading and praise.

NAME_____ DATE_____

13

Keep Movin' On!

What an exciting world we live in! Life itself is a constant set of adjustments, and nothing is static. This brings with it new challenges.

The very nature of life demands some change as we are being forced to reevaluate priorities and accept new challenges for personal growth.

At no time in history has the woman been faced with such an accelerated pattern of change. She has in the last decade, been brought from television to the moon by way of the satellite. She views life ahead in terms of the neutron bomb, futuristic architecture, and the space shuttle.

The information explosion has computerized a person into a set of numbers; body language reveals the woman's hidden aggressions; handwriting tells her secret personality traits. As if that isn't enough, now they have discovered that the posture in which one sleeps, reveals Freudian hangups. Big Deal! It seems that nothing in life is private or sacred to the twentieth century woman.

These cultural changes over the past decade have forced significant differences upon this generation of women. Do you know we are the first women to have a choice, by reason of the "pill," to decide if we do—or do not—wish to have children? The nature of this freedom from childbearing has brought with it certain moral decisions, making it easier to become promiscuous without obvious penalties.

On the surface it looks like a happy-go-lucky kind of living. But the story is not always the same. I wonder if we are aware of the psychological repercussions that are coming from our amoral society. While I would not blame the little round pill for causing a woman to do "anything," I certainly see that it has made it easier for her to do "some things."

Recently, while in the office of my gynecologist, the doctor discussed with me the question of: "What is happening to the new generation of women who have thrown off all moral restraints and who by their so-called freedoms have moved from one partner to another (making the sacredness of sex little more than an animalistic experience on a water bed of convenience)? He told me that the medical profession was concerned: that this "living-together-syndrome," being popularized by extreme groups, was still bringing with it a great aftermath of guilt and deep psychological problems. He observed that, in most cases, the girl of today is looking for security and the stability of a lasting marriage relationship. When I looked over the proposed program, as planned for a three-day symposium by the Medical Association, I was convinced of their concern about our fast-growing problem.

These conditions call for firm convictions on the

part of all women to build strong guidelines for protection against the subtle acceptance of these standards as being "just a part of the society in which we live." The Bible is perfectly clear about the "brevity of life," and makes provisions for living it to its fullest, within the "life cycle." The transgression of God's known laws, that were given to direct our lives, bring with them certain penalties. To live today, as if tomorrow will never come, is to blindfold oneself into a corner of make-believe.

Life's Certain Uncertainties

While all this scientific, medical research has brought with it new demands—offering opportunities for learning growth and giving us the responsibility for our actions—it also has promised us hopes of greater longevity. Women of the early 1920s and 30s could only hope to live, on the average, until they saw their last child leave home and be married. Seldom did one hear of a couple celebrating their golden anniversary, yet it is not uncommon today to find a couple who have been married, not fifty but sixty years. Because a woman is living longer than her forebears, and her childbearing years are shorter (by reason of her choice), she is no longer confined to the home past her mid years. Since this is a youth-oriented society, she may find herself with vitality ready to discover new avenues of self-fulfillment, going back to school, becoming involved with church groups and in community involvements.

Marcia Laswell, psychology professor at Claremont College, in a class lecture referred to the following life cycle changes through which the average woman passes in her married lifetime.

Cycle Changes

1. *"I DO"* and the *DIAPER STAGES* when the woman is busy with her responsibility of a husband, raising children and "wiping dirty noses."

2. *MOTHERING YEARS* of plain hard work, getting the family off to school, maintaining an atmosphere of day-to-day living, and providing support for a husband who is usually trying to work his way to the top of the business ladder.

3. *SHUFFLING YEARS* when her schedule is built around the children's activities, getting one to the ball park on time, attending the P.T.A., and running a "taxi" service for the teen-ager who is just under the age limit for a driver's license.

4. *HALF-AND-HALF YEARS* the first children are out of the house and mother goes back to work to put them through college; the rest of the time is divided between the husband, job, children and home.

5. *CAREER OPPORTUNITIES* are open for the woman to be a full-time wife, and fall in love with her husband all over again. While doing that, she may wish to return to school, take some kind of self-improvement course, or move out into a new and exciting venture within the home.

6. *FREEDOM YEARS* when the woman who has learned how to live, up to this point in the cycle, should not find it difficult to adjust. If she has centered her life around her grandchildren and arthritis, there will be problems! (Those seem to be the two major topics of conversation among this age-level when they get together.)

7. *TIME AND CHARACTER YEARS* when in

retirement the real person lives with the person they have been. The input of life's experiences has become the "seasoning" that provides strength and support for those around them.

What I see happening among many women is a simple refusal to accept these ongoing inevitabilities of life; to recognize that each phase has its own area of adjustments, but . . . it also has advantages!

ILLUSTRATIONS:

A young mother came crying as she told me about her last child having reached kindergarten age. The trauma of sending her offspring off to school, and an empty house with no little ones around, was too much for her to accept. (This was hard for me to understand because I felt the school teacher was doing me a favor when my 'fledglings" waved good-bye at the threshold of the classroom. Fortunately, the mother who talked with me was able to make the adjustment without any problem.)

However, I have seen many mothers who could not live with the feeling that their family was growing away from them. (That is usually caused because the mother has centered her life around the needs of the family, having no identity of her own.) I can understand there is a kind of loneliness about the house, and an uninterrupted silence to which we are unaccustomed. (What a welcome one!) Yet, some of us go through life clinging to each changing cycle as if it were the last—and there were no tomorrows.

Not so!

The same principle applies in the feeling of growing older. I counsel with young women, career girls, who have this kind of "life-is-passing-me-by" sort of feeling. It is as though they are being cheated. Maybe they have not been able to see all of their dreams fulfilled. That doesn't banish the dreams of the future! Most of us never found our Prince Charming riding a white steed (Mine was a young minister in a blue Chevrolet, with monthly installments owing on it.) So what! Neither was I a Cinderella at midnight . . . or any other time.

There are two ways in which to accept disappointments and change. One is to resist it, to become rigidly inflexible and stubbornly fixed until a crisis breaks us; like the straight unyieldedness of an oak tree. Or, we can be like the willow, whose branches bend to the ground from the blowing winds, but are lifted skyward as the storm passes.

Every woman must decide whether to meet these changes or disappointments and face up to them or to try running away. There is no way to get around God's certain uncertainties. What are they?

1. Beauty which is consumed in age   Ps. 39:11
2. Promises made by ruling authority figures   Ps. 146:3
3. Riches that fly away like the wings of an eagle   Prov. 23:5
4. A future that cannot be boasted of, not even the tomorrow   Prov. 27:1
5. Friends that may scatter in time of adversity   John 16:32
6. Life which is considered as a vapor   James 4:14
7. Earthly glory of man as the withering of the grass   1 Pet. 1:24
8. Death and the afterlife Heb. 9:27

Among the above-mentioned things, women seem to be most mentally preoccupied with two of them: the loss of their youthful beauty and death. First, let me say, we can stop neither! Death is a part of living so we must accept that. But, what about the other?

Inner Beauty vs. Outer

No thinking woman takes pride in her sagging wrinkles and aging neckline. But, to become obsessed with the thought of aging is to fight time itself. Outer beauty is always measured by the eye of the beholder. Inner beauty is never, and cannot be hidden by age or circumstance. It is timeless! The tranquility of the inner soul is like an ornament of grace and dignity, growing more beautiful with each passing year. Did not the psalmist speak of this when he said: "For the Lord taketh pleasure in his people: he will beautify the meek with salvation" (Ps. 149:4 KJV.

And, we are told in the New Testament to put on "the ornament of a meek and quiet spirit" (1 Pet. 3:4 KJV).

There is nothing so disappointing, to me, as seeing a well "coiffeured" woman, meticulously dressed, with a lovely face, and perfect figure; only to later discover, beneath all those coverings of beauty, is ugliness and sham.

On the other hand, there is nothing more delightfully refreshing as the woman whose inner strength accentuates her natural beauty. She, too, can and should be the well-combed, groomed lady of her day. One quality does not cancel out the other.

Plan of Action

READ: 1 Pet. 3:4-6

Ask yourself?

When did I last get a new hairdo? Change my style of clothing? Do anything toward self-improvement?

Is my husband, family, others proud of me?

What is my general mental attitude? Is it mostly negative? . . . or is it positive?

If it is negative, why?

READ: Phil. 4:8